SPOTLIGHT

S0-BIG-435

VIRGINIA COAST

KATIE GITHENS

Contents

VIRGINIA COAST

THE COAST

A simple concept—Virginia meets the ocean—is quite complex in reality. Comprising both the state's largest city and towns where the whole population could fit in a school bus, the coast embraces some of Virginia's greatest diversity in both its landscape and its people. Aside from the Atlantic Ocean, its major defining natural feature is the Chesapeake Bay, whose gaping mouth opens onto one of the finest, largest, and busiest natural ports in the world. Around this harbor spreads Hampton Roads, which counts some 1.6 million residents—more than a fifth of Virginia's population.

Rivers divide the inner shore of the Chesapeake Bay into three large "necks" of land. The southernmost one, called the Historic Peninsula, is home to three of the state's most exceptional sites, each within a short drive of the others: Jamestown became the first permanent English settlement in the New World in 1607 when three ships full of settlers sailed up the bay; Yorktown was the site of the decisive final battle of the American Revolution; and a visit to Colonial Williamsburg can make you think the 18th century never really ended.

In stark contrast to all this history is Hampton Roads, officially the Norfolk–Virginia Beach–Newport News Metropolitan Statistical Area. It boasts the world's largest coal-shipping port, privately owned shipyard, and naval facility, and one-third of its workers are employed by the Department of Defense or private defense contractors. Yet around this megalopolis—close enough, in parts, to see its glow at night—are some of the state's most pristine natural acres, covering miles of

HIGHLIGHTS

◖ **Irvington:** This tiny town on the Northern Neck is great for a weekend getaway, with the outstanding trio of the Hope and Glory Inn, the Trick Dog Cafe, and historic Christ Church (page 14).

◖ **Historical Sights of Colonial Williamsburg:** Here, at one of America's most popular family destinations, life in the 18th century is re-created down to bootstraps and belt buckles (page 21).

◖ **Jamestown Island (Colonial National Historical Park):** Jamestown, Yorktown, and the connecting parkway make up this historical park, which spans centuries of history, from the first lasting English settlement in the New World to the final battle of the American Revolution (page 31).

◖ **James River Plantations:** The impressive lineup along the James River includes Shirley Plantation, America's oldest, and Berkeley Plantation, site of one of the first Thanksgivings by European settlers (page 35).

◖ **The Mariners' Museum:** In Newport News, this museum plays host to all things nautical, from scrimshaw to pieces of the famous ironclad, the *Monitor* (page 39).

◖ **NAUTICUS:** The National Maritime Center in Norfolk is a high-tech museum that's as impressive as the 887-foot USS *Wisconsin* berthed next door (page 49).

◖ **Virginia Beach Boardwalk:** This is a scrubbed-up version of the classic beach boardwalk, with lots to do and people to watch (page 61).

◖ **Virginia Aquarium and Marine Science Center:** Check out sharks, turtles, and gentle stingrays at this outstanding aquarium, one of the best of its kind in the country (page 62).

◖ **Chincoteague National Wildlife Refuge and Assateague Island:** At the northern end of the Eastern Shore, this refuge at one end of wild Assateague Island is home to the world-famous wild ponies, rounded up every year by volunteer firemen (page 85).

◖ **Tangier Island:** A boat trip to Tangier Island, isolated in the middle of the Chesapeake Bay, is a unique cultural experience and almost a trip back in time — life here hasn't changed much in decades (page 88).

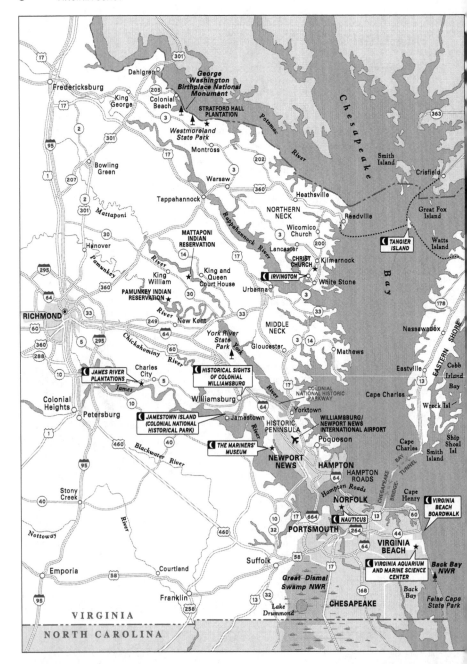

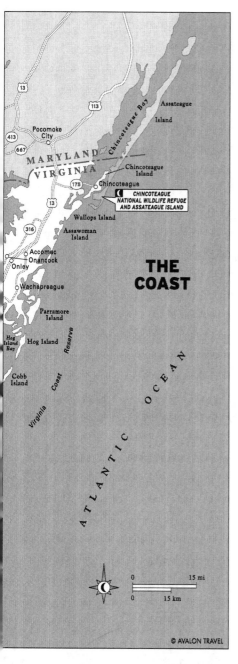

undisturbed shoreline, barrier islands, swamps, marshes, and estuaries.

PLANNING YOUR TIME

Because it's a little less convenient to get around by car, what with all the rivers and bays and estuaries everywhere you turn, Virginia's coast really takes a week or more to explore thoroughly. If you have less time than that you should head down the Historic Peninsula to Hampton Roads, but be warned that most of the millions of people who visit this part of the state every year will be doing the same. Heading out the peninsula from Richmond, don't miss the **historic plantations** along the James River and all the fun stuff in and near Williamsburg, including **Busch Gardens Europe, Colonial Williamsburg,** and the **Colonial National Historical Park,** which encompasses Jamestown and Yorktown. Each deserves a full day.

Along with plentiful nightlife, restaurants, and hotels, the Hampton Roads area offers some of Virginia's most outstanding museums, including **The Mariners' Museum** in Newport News, **NAUTICUS** in Norfolk, and the **Virginia Aquarium and Marine Science Center** in Virginia Beach. (The latter also boasts dozens of miles of beaches and a classic boardwalk.) Any of these cities can serve as a home base for exploring the area. A few out-of-the-way destinations worth a stop are the charming town of **Irvington** on the Northern Neck and culturally unique **Tangier Island** out in the bay. In a weekend you can visit Tangier and the wild ponies at the **Chincoteague National Wildlife Refuge** at the northern end of the pastoral Eastern Shore.

Access

The only Virginia interstate that heads seaward is I-64 from Richmond, threading the Historic Peninsula as it runs east to Williamsburg and the Hampton Roads area. U.S. 17 leaves Fredericksburg for the Middle Neck, where it crosses U.S. 360 before crossing the York River at Yorktown. The Northern and Middle Necks each have their own backbone: Route 3 runs the length of the former, and U.S. 17 skewers

The Virginia Aquarium in Virginia Beach draws 620,000 visitors per year.

the latter. U.S. 360 runs from Richmond across both to Reedville.

Farther south, U.S. 460 connects Petersburg with Suffolk near Hampton Roads, and U.S. 58 rolls east from Emporia more or less along the North Carolina state line toward Portsmouth. Two of the most scenic ways to reach the coast are Route 5, which passes half a dozen James River plantations southeast of Richmond, and U.S. 13 down the length of the Eastern Shore from Maryland.

Northern Neck

Reaching bayward between broad, patient rivers, the Necks evoke the Piedmont, but with a shoreside twist. A hazy light filters across the flat farmland, where the odor of freshly mown fields mixes with the brackish breeze off the Chesapeake Bay. Talk at the local store is as likely to be about fixing outboards as about keeping a Chevy running. Full of local color, it's more rural than much of central Virginia. Visitors come for quiet walks, fishing, boating, and shopping from spring to fall. In the off-season, many towns shut down much of their tourist facilities, so calling ahead is always a good idea.

Information and Tours

For more information on this part of the coast, contact the **Northern Neck Tourism Council** in Warsaw (804/333-1919 or 800/393-6180, www.northernneck.org). **Northern Neck Heritage Tours** (804/580-5179, www.nnht .com) offers guided, customizable historical and ecological tours of the area and can help set up accommodations and food, as well as logistical support for paddlers and bird-watchers.

GEORGE WASHINGTON BIRTHPLACE NATIONAL MONUMENT

The father of this country squalled into the light on February 22, 1732, on Pope's Creek Plantation, on the southern bank of the Potomac. It doesn't seem like a bad place to spend the first three and a half years of one's life, here among the trees where a meandering creek empties into the river. Although the building in which Washington was born is gone, an outline in crushed oyster shells shows where it stood, next to a reconstructed farm complete with outbuildings and animal pens.

Pleasant paths lead from the visitors center to the Memorial House, which contains an original tea table. George's father, grandfather, and great-grandfather lie in the family cemetery nearby. Rangers offer talks on the hour, and costumed interpreters manage the working farm in season, providing a window into 18th-century life in the Tidewater. A nature trail continues to a picnic area, and at the end of the road a beach on the Potomac. The monument (804/224-1732, www.nps.gov/gewa, 9 A.M.–5 P.M. daily, $4 pp) is on Route 204 off Route 3.

WESTMORELAND STATE PARK

Ancient marine fossils trapped in Horsehead Cliffs attest to the age (more than 127 million years) of the sediments that make up this peninsula between the Rappahannock and Potomac Rivers. It was set aside in 1936 as one of Virginia's first six state parks. Behind the beach and steep riverside bluffs stretch 1,299 acres of meadows and forest populated by beavers, hawks, and turkeys. Six miles of easy and moderate hiking trails lead to Rock Spring Pond and an observation tower over Fossil Beach.

The park (804/493-8821, www.dcr.virginia.gov/state_parks/wes.shtml, dawn–dusk daily, $3 weekdays, $4 weekends) is on Route 347 off Route 3 and has seven miles of hiking trails, a swimming pool, picnic areas, and a playground. You can spend the night in one of 26 camping cabins ($57–112), open year-round, or at one of the park's 133 campsites ($20–25), open March–December. The Potomac River Retreat can hold 16 people in two fully contained living areas and has deck areas facing the Potomac River ($250–360). A seasonal camp store sells supplies and rents kayaks and pedalboats. The visitors center (noon–5 P.M. Wed.–Sun. in season, weekends only May and

kayaks at Westmoreland State Park

WESTMORELAND BERRY FARM AND ORCHARD

You can pick your own raspberries, blackberries, blueberries, and strawberries at this 80-acre farm along the Rappahannock. Or you can just stop by to sample more than a dozen seasonal fruits, including apricots, peaches, cherries, apples, plums, and pumpkins. The plump red strawberries grown at Westmoreland have been known to draw lines dozens deep at northern Virginia farmers markets in early summer, so why not beat the crowds and pick them yourself? A snack bar serves fruit sundaes, frozen yogurt, and other toothsome mouthfuls. (Look for goats clambering about the raised platforms and ramps of the aerial "goat walk.")

The **farm** (804/224-9171 or 800/997-2377, www.westmorelandberryfarm.com) is southwest of Oak Grove on Route 638, reached from Route 3 via Route 634. It's open during growing season (May–Oct.) 9 A.M.–5 P.M. Monday-Saturday, 10 A.M.-5 P.M. Sunday. Check out its website for a harvest schedule and a list of annual events.

Sept.–Oct.) has exhibits on the natural history of the area, including shark's teeth. Ask about kayak trips along the Horsehead Cliffs on weekends May–October ($16–22).

STRATFORD HALL PLANTATION

Robert E. Lee, the Northern Neck's other famous son, was born on an estate his family had occupied for almost a century. In the late 1730s on a bluff near the Potomac, Thomas Lee built a huge mansion shaped like an *H* in honor of his wife, Hanna. In 1782 his nephew, Henry, moved in and married Annie Hill Carter of Shirley Plantation. Henry went on to make a name for himself in the Revolutionary War as Harry "Light-Horse" Lee. But on January 19, 1807, just four years before Henry lost his fortune in land speculation and moved the family to Alexandria, Annie gave birth to a son who was destined for even greater fame: Robert Edward.

The Great House, one of the most majestic buildings in the state, looks like a brick castle set back a short distance from the river. Sixteen fireplaces and numerous 17th- and 18th-century furnishings fill the cavernous interior. These include many Lee heirlooms, such as a 1660 clock and the crib in which Robert slept as a baby. Notice the 17-foot "inverted tray" ceiling in the Great Hall, and ask about the fireplace angels to which Robert bid good-bye as the family was packing to move. Downstairs are servants' quarters, the original kitchen, bedrooms, and a schoolroom where the teacher slept.

Stratford Hall (804/493-8038, www.stratfordhall.org, 9:30 A.M.–4 P.M. daily, $10 adults, $5 children) is on Route 214 off Route 3. A reception center houses a museum, where you can learn about things like estimating the age of clay pipes by the diameter of their stems, and a gift shop selling fresh-ground corn and oats from the estate's fully functional mill. Stratford has two guesthouses, each with a full kitchen, with 20 rooms between them for $132 d. There's also a log-cabin dining room serving a hearty plantation lunch daily. Three miles of nature trails explore the working plantation's 1,700 rural acres. Annual events include Robert E. Lee's birthday (January 19), African-American Heritage Day (usually the last weekend in February), and a traditional Thanksgiving feast.

REEDVILLE

Founded in 1867 ("by Northerners," grumbles one pamphlet), this small city was reportedly the richest per capita in the country around World War I, thanks to the abundant menhaden fishing in Chesapeake Bay. Today, boats sit in the driveways of tidy houses along Main Street (Rte. 360), which dead-ends at the water along Millionaires' Row, named for a succession of gorgeous Victorian mansions. Reedville is also one gateway to Tangier Island in the Chesapeake Bay.

Sights

The **Reedville Fisherman's Museum** (504 Main St., 804/453-6529, www.rfmuseum .org, 10:30 A.M.–4:30 P.M. daily May–Oct., by appt. only Jan.–Mar., otherwise weekends only in off-season, $5 adults) has been set up in the 1875 Walker House along Main Street just before Millionaires' Row. Displays of ship models, photos, tools, and artwork lead visitors to traditional boats such as a crabbing skiff moored to the rear dock.

Recreation

Captain Billy's Charters (804/580-7292, www.captbillyscharters.com) runs fishing trips aboard the 46-foot *Liquid Assets II* out of the Ingram Bay Marina, near Wicomico Church, for $650 for up to six people. Fishing trips for rockfish, striped bass, and tuna cost more. Other fishing charter options include Capt. Jim Hardy's *Ranger II* (804/453-6635) and Jim Conner's *Jeannie C* (804/453-4021). All outfits provide gear and will even clean your fish for you.

Events

The opening of the fishing season is celebrated during the **Blessing of the Fleet** the first weekend in May. In mid-September, the **Antique Boat Parade** floats down Reedville's Cockrells Creek. The traditional **RFM Oyster Roast** takes place the second Saturday in November and packs tiny Reedville with crowds hankering for tons of seafood. The Reedville Fisherman's Museum also hosts a **family boatbuilding weekend** each year, though dates vary. Contact the museum for information on all events.

Accommodations

The Gables (804/453-5209, www.thegablesbb .com) occupies the unmistakable brick mansion at the end of Main Street, built in the late 1800s by a local captain who brought the bricks by schooner from New England. (The boat's three masts were used in the construction.) One room in the mansion and four in the nearby Coach House Inn (where you'll find the ice cream parlor) are $90–175. Two luxury suites in the well-named Waterside Cottage, built in 2006, run $195–235. In the nearby village of Fleeton is the **Fleeton Fields B&B** (2783 Fleeton Rd., 804/453-5014 or 800/497-8215, www.fleetonfields.com), with three suites with a view of rose-filled gardens and the bay for $150–195.

The **Chesapeake Bay Camp-Resort** (382 Campground Rd., 804/453-3430) is located 2.5 miles northeast of the intersection of Route 652 and U.S. 360 and has 82 campsites for $40–50, as well as cabins for $55–110. Rowboats and canoes are rented here, of course.

Food

Down at the end of Main Street by the marina is **The Crazy Crab** (902 Main St., 804/453-6789, dinner Tues.–Fri., lunch and dinner Sat.–Sun., weekends only in off-season, $14–26), with an outdoor deck, plenty of wine, and daily chef specials of seafood, steak, and chicken. The deli counter at **Cockrell's Creek Seafood Deli** (south on Seaboard Rd. off Fleeton Rd., 804/453-6326, 10 A.M.–5 P.M. Mon.–Sat. in season) sells scallops, shrimp, crabs, and other marine delicacies to go or to eat at its picnic area. Sandwiches are $5–6, and full dinners are $10–15.

Tours and Transportation

Smith Island Cruise (804/453-3430, www .cruisetosmithisland.com) offers narrated day tours to Smith Island, Maryland, in the 150-person *Spirit of the Chesapeake*. Departing at 10 A.M. from the Chesapeake Bay Camp-Resort in Reedville (daily May–Oct.), the tours allow time to explore Ewell Island, one of three fishing villages, each on its own island, that make up Smith Island. The trip returns at 3:45 P.M. and costs $25 adults, $13 children. Reservations are required.

Day trips to Tangier Island and lunch cruises up the Rappahannock to the Ingleside Plantation Winery are only two of the trips offered by **Tangier & Rappahannock Cruises** (804/453-2628, www.tangiercruise.com). The

Chesapeake Breeze leaves daily at 10 A.M. for Tangier Island, returning about 4 P.M., for $25 adults, $13 children, with an optional lunch. Reservations are recommended during the summer. Narrated lunch and dinner tours aboard a paddle wheeler in Fredericksburg are also offered ($26–45 adults, $16.50–27 children), with onboard dancing on Friday and Saturday. Boats leave May–October from the Buzzard's Point Marina, reached by taking a right before Reedville onto Fairport Road (Rte. 626), followed by a left onto Buzzard Point Road.

◖ IRVINGTON
Christ Church
The showpiece of this small fishing town is a monolithic house of worship completed in 1735 by Robert "King" Carter. One of the few unaltered Colonial churches in the country, it features a high arching ceiling, shoulder-high walls between family-sized pew "boxes," and a three-level pulpit, although it has no bell tower. Services are still held here from June to Labor Day, and the church building (804/438-6855, www.christchurch1735.org) is open 8:30 A.M.–4 P.M. Monday–Friday year-round, and 10 A.M.–4 P.M. Saturday and 2–5 P.M. Sunday April–November. A reception center with a small museum is open 10 A.M.–4 P.M. Monday–Saturday and 2–5 P.M. Sunday April–November. Suggested donation is $5. The church is on Christ Church Road (Rte. 646) off Route 200 just north of town.

Events
Come by the first Saturday in September for the **Irvington Stomp** (www.irvingtonstomp .com), celebrating the annual grape harvest at the White Fences Vineyard with music and the crowning of the King and Queen of the Stomp. Tickets are $10 for adults, $5 for children 6–16.

Accommodations and Food
In 1890, a schoolhouse opened in an old Methodist church near the center of Irvington. Today the building houses ◖ **The Hope and Glory Inn** (65 Tavern Rd., 804/438-5362 or 800/497-8228, www.hopeandglory.com). This award-winning place is decked out with folk art and a large central lobby where classrooms once echoed with children's voices. If the seven bedrooms in the schoolhouse ($175–245 weekdays, $195–290 weekends) are full, there are also six charming guest cottages ($240–430) out back, near an enclosed outdoor bath with claw-foot tub, shower, and sink. The English cottage garden features a moon patch that blooms in the evening. They've also opened a handful of "tents" (read: super-cute cottages) at the nearby White Fences Vineyard. These three-bedroom places have screened porches and outdoor showers, and start at $310–385 for one-bedroom usage.

The chic little **Trick Dog Cafe** (4357 Irvington Rd., 804/438-6363) was named for a dog statue in the entrance that was rescued, blackened but unhurt, from the great town fire of 1917. (Petting it is supposed to bring good luck.) They serve tasty bites like tuna tartare and excellent crab cakes ($18–25) for dinner Tuesday–Saturday. Irvington has been called a place "where Mayberry meets Manhattan," a reputation no doubt cultivated by the Trick Dog—though it could just be the green apple martinis going to a travel writer's head.

Along Carter's Creek you'll find the first-class **Tides Inn** (480 King Carter Dr., 804/438-5000 or 800/843-3746, www.tidesinn.com). This all-inclusive getaway has been rated among the top 50 in the country by *Travel + Leisure* magazine. It features two restaurants, a spa, the top-rated Golden Eagle golf course, a sandy beach, a saltwater pool, and a marina. Rooms start at $260. If all the water in every direction has you itching to learn to sail, contact its certified sailing school (804/438-9300, www.sailingschool.net).

Information
Contact the town of Irvington (804/438-6230, www.irvingtonva.org) for more information.

White Stone
Just minutes from Irvington, this village is home to the **White Stone Wine and Cheese Co.** (572

Rappahannock Dr., 804/435-2000) on Route 3, offering the largest local wine selection and gourmet soups and sandwiches in a small café. Another nearby option for a gourmet breakfast or lunch is **Willaby's** (453 Rappahannock Dr., 804/435-0000), serving fancy burgers and tasty desserts for lunch ($5–10) Monday–Saturday. **Rocket Billy's** (851 Rappahannock Dr., 804/435-7040, 6 A.M.–3 P.M. Mon.–Sat.) serves excellent seafood, including crab cakes, soft-shell-crab sandwiches, and bisque, from a red, white, and blue trailer.

Middle Neck

URBANNA

One of 20 port towns established by a 1680 Act of Assembly, Urbanna was named for England's Queen Anne (as was Annapolis, Maryland). The town has weathered pirate attacks and three wars during its centuries as a tobacco export center and fishing village. Watermen still unload their day's catch on wharves shared by recreational boaters and anglers, only a short walk from Victorian homes on the National Register of Historic Places.

Sights

Opened in 1876, the **R. S. Bristow Store** (Virginia St. at Cross St., 804/758-2210) once sold patent medicines, live chickens, and wood by the cord. More than 125 years later it's still in business, selling clothes, gifts, and household goods. There's a shoe section where the post office used to be and an old-fashioned rolling ladder to reach the higher shelves. The nearby **courthouse building** dates to 1748, making it the oldest structure in Urbanna. It has served various functions over the years, shifting from a church to Confederate Civil War barracks to its present role as a women's club headquarters.

Events

Held on the first weekend in November, the **Urbanna Oyster Festival** (804/758-0368, www.urbannaoysterfestival.com) draws nearly 75,000 people with a firemen's parade, food and crafts, oyster-shucking contest, and the crowning of the Oyster Festival Queen and Little Miss Spat. It's been going strong for more than 50 years.

Accommodations

The **Atherston Hall B&B** (250 Prince George St., 804/758-2809, www.atherstonhall.com, $115–150) was originally the home of a 19th-century schooner captain. It offers three rooms, a suite, homemade granola and other breakfast offerings, afternoon tea, and day sailing trips aboard the *Victorious, Tregony,* or *Harry.*

A pair of former restaurateurs have turned an 1870s Victorian mansion into the **Inn at Urbanna Creek** (210 Watling St., 804/758-4661, www.innaturbannacreek.com, $95–160). Choose from three rooms and a separate cottage with vaulted ceilings and a private deck and garden. Rates include a full breakfast.

Waterfront campsites at the **Bethpage Camp Resort** (804/758-4349, www.bethpage camp.com), about 15 miles west near the intersection of Routes 17 and 684, are $40–55 with full hookups. This huge place has two pools, a tennis court, a grocery store, and a marina. Open April–mid-November.

Seven miles away in Church View, at the intersection of Routes 17 and 602, is the **Dragon Run Inn** (35 Ware Bridge Rd., 804/758-5719, www.dragon-run-inn.com). The former farmhouse was built in 1913 with cypress from a nearby swamp. The four rooms (whimsically named Dog, Cow, Pig, and Sheep) are each $100–150 per night, and meals can be arranged with advance reservations.

Food

For such a small town, Urbanna has no shortage of cafés. **Marshall's Drug Store** (50 Cross St., 804/758-5344) offers an authentic old-fashioned lunch counter with real milk shakes, and the **Virginia Street Café** (201 Virginia St., 804/758-3798, all meals daily) serves simple but satisfying food.

Café Mojo (230 Virginia St., 804/758-4141, dinner Thurs.–Sat.) is more upscale, serving up eclectic surf, turf, and pasta entrées ($12–16) with European and Mexican influences and a funky bar with live music.

Two miles north of town is **Something Different** (3617 Old Virginia St., 804/758-8004, 10 A.M.–6 P.M. Wed.–Fri., 8 A.M.–6 P.M. Sat., 8 A.M.–3 P.M. Sun.), a country store and deli serving up fresh-ground coffee, homemade ice cream, and some of the best North Carolina–style barbecue around.

Information

For more on Urbanna, contact the town offices at 45 Cross Street (804/758-2613, www .urbanna.com).

INDIAN RESERVATIONS

A museum on the 1,200-acre **Pamunkey Indian Reservation** (804/843-4792, www .pamunkey.net, 10 A.M.–4 P.M. Tues.–Sat., 1–5 P.M. Sun., $2.50 adults, $1.25 children) traces the history of the largest chiefdom of the Powhatan confederacy, established in 1607. Extensive displays include beautiful ceremonial garments and a collection of mean-looking weapons, including a huge collection of handmade flint points. Several local potters have formed a guild to begin reviving traditional methods, and their wares are for sale in the museum shop. To find it, take Route 633 or Route 626 south from Route 30, then follow the signs.

Officially designated in 1658, the **Mattaponi Reservation** (http://indians.vip-net.org/tribes/mattaponi.cfm) has been whittled down to only 150 acres. It's located off Route 30 opposite the Pamunkey Reservation via Route 626 or Route 640 and hosts an annual powwow in mid-June, with dancing, drumming, food, and crafts ($5 pp). Every year the tribal chief presents the governor of Virginia with a gift of peace in accordance with original treaties.

Colonial Williamsburg

America's largest and most popular living-history museum re-creates the Colonial capital as it was on November 11, 1775, the tense eve of the Revolutionary War. One of the most ambitious historical projects ever, this isn't just a few restored farms or households—this is an entire town brought back to life and inhabited by people portraying a cadre of craftspeople, slaves, merchants, and aristocrats.

It may not be everyone's cup of tea (or ale), but Colonial Williamsburg is a remarkable feat, the product of decades of research, experimentation, and refinement. The realism—aside from the hordes of tourists—is amazing. Horse-drawn carriages clop past a merchant arguing with his neighbor over the best course of political action, while nonplussed ducks wander down a dusty lane where a smith stands sweating over his forge. Best of all, you can even take part in it yourself. Join a tipsy Colonial gentleman in singing tavern songs, learn the finer points of baking apple fritters from his wife, immerse yourself in the latest findings at an archaeological dig, or sit on a courthouse jury to decide whether a pig thief deserves a flogging or just a day in the stocks.

Children especially love the "living" aspect of Williamsburg, and get a kick out of rolling hoops across the Palace Green in three-cornered hats or taking lessons from the Dancing Master in the Governor's Palace. Colonial Williamsburg has done an enviable job of marketing itself as the ultimate family destination, covering both the educational and entertainment angles—and a million visitors a year would argue it has been successful.

Costumed interpreters in Colonial Williamsburg dress the part and often present their characters in the first person.

HISTORY

Rural acreage known as Middle Plantation got a rude awakening when it was picked as the site for the new Colonial capital in 1699. The planter aristocracy of the day had decided it needed a more sophisticated spot for the business of governing and socializing than damp Jamestown, and this site, near the newly established Royal College of William and Mary, seemed suitable.

Plans were immediately set in motion to transform a scattering of plantation buildings into a capital fit for one of Britain's oldest colonies. First to be laid out was Duke of Gloucester Street, 100 feet wide and almost one mile long, from William and Mary's Wren Building at one end to the capitol building at the other. A grassy mall led to the Governor's Palace.

The town quickly became the cultural and political center of Virginia and the focus of Colonial America's most fashionable social scene. As a ceremonial city with little manufacturing base, Williamsburg swelled during "Public Times" in April and October. Rural gentry rode in from their plantations to attend sessions of the House of Burgesses and Governor's Council, delighting in a social whirl that, they said, rivaled London's. Countless balls, races, and a fair competed for attention with performances by English actors and musicians in one of the earliest theaters in America.

Williamsburg welcomed some impressive names during its heyday, including George Washington, George Mason, and Patrick Henry. Thomas Jefferson first arrived in the early 1760s as a student at William and Mary and returned later as a member of the House of Burgesses. In 1719, 13 pirates from the ship of the notorious Edward Teach (Blackbeard) were tried and condemned to death in the General Court chamber in the capitol building. A decade later, Williamsburg boasted the first successful printing press in the colony, followed soon after by its first newspaper and paper mill.

Patrick Henry defied the British Stamp Act

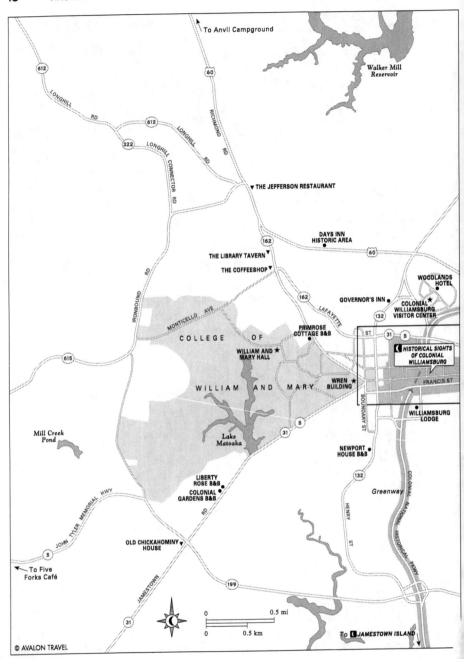

To Anvil Campground

Walker Mill Reservoir

612

60

LONGHILL RD

612

322

LONGHILL CONNECTOR RD

LONGHILL RD

RICHMOND RD

▼ THE JEFFERSON RESTAURANT

DAYS INN
HISTORIC AREA
●

162

THE LIBRARY TAVERN ▼

THE COFFEESHOP ▼

60

162

LAFAYETTE

GOVERNOR'S INN
●

WOODLANDS
HOTEL
●

COLONIAL ★
WILLIAMSBURG
VISITOR CENTER

RD

IRONBOUND RD

MONTICELLO AVE

COLLEGE   OF

PRIMROSE
COTTAGE B&B ▼
●

WILLIAM AND ★
MARY HALL

132

ST

31   5

**▐ HISTORICAL SIGHTS
OF COLONIAL
WILLIAMSBURG**

615

WILLIAM   AND   MARY

WREN ★
BUILDING

FRANCIS ST

BOUNDARY ST

WILLIAMSBURG
LODGE
●

Mill Creek
Pond

*Lake
Matoaka*

31

5

NEWPORT
HOUSE B&B ●

LIBERTY
ROSE B&B ●

COLONIAL ●
GARDENS B&B

RD

132

Greenway

HENRY ST

COLONIAL NATIONAL HISTORICAL PKWY

JOHN TYLER MEMORIAL HWY

OLD CHICKAHOMINY ▼
HOUSE

5

← To Five
Forks Café

JAMESTOWN RD

199

31

0   0.5 mi

0   0.5 km

To ▐ *JAMESTOWN ISLAND*

© AVALON TRAVEL

WILLIAMSBURG

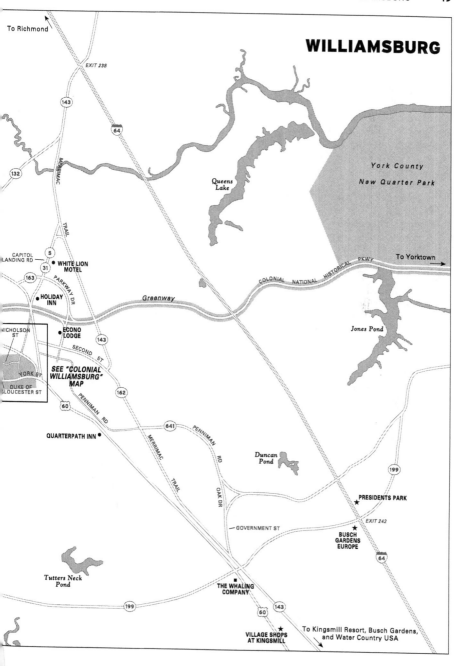

To Richmond

EXIT 238

143

64

MERRIMAC

132

TRAIL

Queens
Lake

York County
New Quarter Park

CAPITOL
LANDING RD

5

31 WHITE LION
MOTEL

163

PARKWAY DR

HOLIDAY
INN

Greenway

COLONIAL NATIONAL HISTORICAL PKWY

To Yorktown

NICHOLSON
ST

ECONO
LODGE

143

SECOND ST

Jones Pond

YORK ST

DUKE OF
GLOUCESTER ST

SEE "COLONIAL
WILLIAMSBURG"
MAP

162

60

PENNIMAN RD

QUARTERPATH INN

641

PENNIMAN RD

Duncan
Pond

199

MERRIMAC

TRAIL

OAK DR

PRESIDENTS PARK

EXIT 242

GOVERNMENT ST

BUSCH
GARDENS
EUROPE

64

Tutters Neck
Pond

THE WHALING
COMPANY

199

60 143

VILLAGE SHOPS
AT KINGSMILL

To Kingsmill Resort, Busch Gardens,
and Water Country USA

in his "Caesar-Brutus" speech to the House of Burgesses on May 30, 1765, throwing sparks ever closer to the fuse of revolution. When Royal Governor Botetourt dissolved the House of Burgesses as it was about to vote to boycott British goods in 1769, its members simply reassembled at the Raleigh tavern and voted there. On May 6, 1776, the fifth Virginia Convention met in Williamsburg to declare Virginia an independent commonwealth, and four years later the capital was moved to Richmond to escape the invading British.

British, Continental, and French forces all billeted on the city's grassy lawns during the Revolutionary War, buying goods from local merchants and providing temporary relief from an economic slump that continued into the 19th century. Restoration began in the 1920s at the instigation of Rev. Dr. W. A. R. Goodwin, rector of the historic Bruton Parish Church. Bankrolled by no less than John D. Rockefeller Jr. (who signed documents anonymously as "David's father"), the plan met with some local resistance until residents realized it was probably the best thing to happen to the city in 150 years.

Exhaustive research in libraries and museums in Europe and America uncovered documents, drawings, and maps detailing Williamsburg's faded glory. More than 450 buildings were torn down, 91 were built, and 67 Colonial structures restored (with their inhabitants allowed to stay on for life).

Eighty-eight original buildings have been meticulously restored on 301 acres. More than 500 other structures have been rebuilt as closely as possible to their original specifications, surrounded by 90 acres of greens and gardens and a 2,800-acre buffer zone against further development. Restoration is constantly being refined as new archaeological information comes to light, from hearth-stone material to hand-painted wallpaper designs.

VISITING COLONIAL WILLIAMSBURG

If you don't plan ahead, visiting Colonial Williamsburg can be an exercise in patience. Reservations for hotels and special events are essential during peak periods (April, May, July, August, October, late November, and December), and early morning is always the best time to visit the more popular stops, such as the Governor's Palace and capitol building.

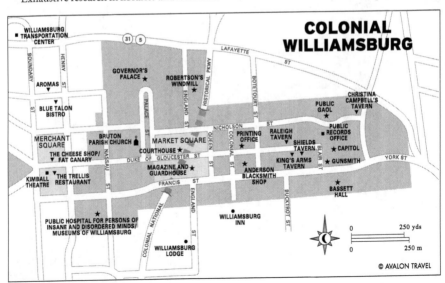

weather vane on a home in
Colonial Williamsburg

You can do the highlights in one day, even a single tiring morning, but a much better plan is to leave yourself a few days to wander the back lanes, chat with the interpreters, and linger over a pint at one of the taverns.

Williamsburg is open 365 days a year, and hours are generally 9 A.M.–5 P.M. daily, but vary with the season. Restaurants and taverns bustle until after dark, and the streets are always free to wander, but you'll need to buy passes to enter the historic buildings. Get information, buy tickets, and make reservations for dining and lodging through the **Colonial Williamsburg Foundation** (800/447-8679, www.history.org).

First stop is the **visitors center** off U.S. 60 bypass and the Colonial Parkway just east of Route 132. Ticket lines can take a while, so you might want to designate a volunteer to wait while everyone else in your party catches the 35-minute orientation film, *Williamsburg— The Story of a Patriot.*

Admission passes come in a few different versions. You can always upgrade to the next level by paying the price difference, and all tickets can be purchased online though the foundation's website. The **1-Day Basic Pass** ($36 adults, $18 children 6–17) gives admission to the town core, including the Capitol, trade shops, and more (it excludes the Governor's Palace Tour). The **1-Day Plus Pass** ($46 adults, $23 children 6–17) adds admission to the Governor's Palace. The **Annual Pass** ($58 adults, $29 children 6–17) provides year-round access and a 25 percent discount on most Colonial Evening Programs. If you stay at one of the Colonial Williamsburg hotels, you can get a **hotel guest ticket** for $30 adults/$15 children, which covers general admission to the historic area. Some evening programs, including music, dancing, and theater performances, require advance reservations and separate admission. With any ticket, you'll receive a copy of the brochure *This Week,* which contains a map and details on the week's events.

The Colonial Williamsburg Foundation has concocted several discount **vacation packages** involving food, lodging, seasonal events, and admission to certain attractions. Contact the foundation for details.

◖ Historical Sights

The mammoth **Governor's Palace** building was constructed 1708–1722 to symbolize the power of the Crown in the colonies. Thomas Jefferson and Patrick Henry stepped through the door as the capital's first two governors, shortly before it burned to its foundation in 1781. The restored building is the single most popular in Colonial Williamsburg, receiving 650,000 visitors annually, so try to get there early in the day.

Shaped like a bulbous *H,* the brick **Capitol** is a reconstruction of the original structure finished in 1705 and burned in 1747. George Washington, among other notables, polished his oratory in the House of Burgesses, the lower elected body that sent proposed laws to the Council for consideration. Interpreters explain how jury duty today is a garden party compared to what it was in the 18th century, when juries were denied heat, food, and water in order to encourage a speedy verdict.

Speaking of verdicts, many a criminal quaked at the sight of the cupola and weather vane atop Williamsburg's **Courthouse,** where severe punishment followed quick judgment. Visitors can take part in the dispensation of Colonial justice on either side of the docket—as a member of the jury or a defendant. Punishments are optional. Across the street, weapons and 60,000 pounds of gunpowder were once stored in the octagonal **Magazine and Guardhouse,** built in 1715 on Duke of Gloucester Street.

One of the country's oldest Episcopal houses of worship, **Bruton Parish Church** (757/229-2891, www.brutonparish.org) stands at the foot of Palace Green, built in 1715. The walls and windows are original. It's not officially part of Colonial Williamsburg, and services are still held here; contact the church for visiting hours.

Offenders and the merely offensive, from pirates and runaway slaves to Tory sympathizers and the insane, all enjoyed the hospitality of Williamsburg's **Public Gaol,** or jail, as we call it today. Built in 1704, it was used until 1910 and has been restored to its 1720s appearance. Miserable barred cells still hold the little extras—manacles, leg irons, and the like—that made every stay special.

Those with mental disorders found themselves in the unfortunate care of Williamsburg's **Public Hospital for Persons of Insane and Disordered Minds** (11 A.M.–6 P.M. daily), the first facility in the country to care for the mentally ill. In the 18th century, insanity was considered a conscious choice, so along with the progressive therapies like sports and music, patients were also kept in cages, dunked in water, and held in manacles to "convince" them to mend their mindset.

Master craftspeople, many of whom have served multiyear apprenticeships, practice Colonial-era crafts at dozens of shops and exhibits throughout the historic area. At the **gunsmith** house, an armorer explains the intricacies of a flintlock musket. You can watch handbills and newspapers being printed on an 18th-century press in the **Printing Office.** One of the best areas to watch demonstrations is near **Robertson's Windmill** (between the Governor's Palace and Randolph House), where coopers build casks and carpenters plane boards for the latest restoration. A shoemaker, silversmith, saddlemaker, and wigmaker operate along **Duke of Gloucester Street** (and elsewhere you can catch a milliner, wheelwright, and blacksmith at work). Stop by the **Pasteur and Galt Apothecary Shop** for a disquieting display of the medical knowledge (or ignorance) of the time. Then visit **R. Charlton's Coffeeshop** for a sip of steaming coffee or hot chocolate.

College of William and Mary

America's second-oldest college (757/221-400, www.wm.edu) was chartered on February 8, 1693, by King William III and Queen Mary II, consisting of three buildings in the angle formed by Richmond and Jamestown

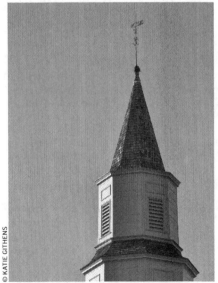

© KATIE GITHENS

steeple of the Bruton Parish Church, circa 1715

Roads. The **Wren Building** was named for Sir Christopher Wren, though he probably didn't design it, and is the oldest academic building in the country still in use (1695). It's been restored to its 1776 appearance. To either side stand the **President's House,** still in use, and the **Brafferton,** originally built as an Indian School.

The college severed ties with Great Britain in 1776 and soon became the first school in the United States to have branches of law and modern languages and operate under an honor system. Thomas Jefferson, James Monroe, and John Tyler are among its more prestigious alumni. The school became state-supported in 1906 and went coeducational in 1918. Today it counts close to 8,000 students, most of whom take advantage of one of the top undergraduate programs in the country taught by more than 667 faculty.

Some 3,000 works of art dating to 1732 are displayed in the **Muscarelle Museum of Art** (757/221-2700, www.wm.edu/muscarelle, 10 A.M.–5 P.M. Tues.–Fri., noon–4 P.M. Sat.–Sun., $5) in Lamberson Hall on Jamestown Road.

OTHER SIGHTS
The Museums of Colonial Williamsburg

A gift of $14 million (the largest in Williamsburg's history) from DeWitt Wallace, the owner of *Reader's Digest,* funded construction of the modern **Wallace Decorative Arts Museum** (325 W. Francis St., 757/229-1000, 10 A.M.–7 P.M. daily, until 5 P.M. in off-season). Entered through the Public Hospital at Francis and North Henry Streets, the museum houses an astonishing collection of 10,000 objects from England and America. Furniture, paintings, ceramics, textiles, silver, and glass on display date to the 17th and 18th centuries. Highlights in the Masterworks Gallery upstairs include a Charles Wilson Peale portrait of George Washington and a case clock made for King William III in 1699. The **Museum Cafe** serves light sandwiches, salads, soups, and wine for lunch.

The world-class **Abby Aldrich Rockefeller Folk Art Museum** (10 A.M.–7 P.M. daily, until 5 P.M. in off-season) houses everything from toys and weather vanes to painted furniture and tinware, ranging in age from the 1730s to the present. The 10,400-square-foot museum was the passion of John D. Rockefeller's wife, one of the first collectors to search out untutored rural artists in the 1920s and 1930s. Her collection shows that true inspiration can have the most humble beginnings. Notice the ship carvings and embroidered mourning pictures.

Presidents Park

A more unusual way to absorb history awaits at this 10-acre park near Water Country USA. Opened in 2004, Presidents Park (211 Water Country Pkwy., 800/588-4327, www .presidentspark.org, 10 A.M.–4 P.M. daily, to 5 P.M. Mar.–May, to 7 P.M. June–Aug., $12.75 adults, $8 children) displays white concrete busts of 43 U.S. presidents. These aren't your everyday busts—each is 18–20 feet tall and weighs around 7,000 pounds. Signs near each one list biographical details, and the overall effect is entertainingly quirky, with educational overtones.

ENTERTAINMENT AND RECREATION
Historical Diversions

Colonial Williamsburg offers a full roster of activities by day and night, from guided walking tours of the historic area to an evening of Vivaldi at the Palace of the Governors. Some events, such as a candlelit walk around the city's haunted spots, are scheduled. Others just happen—as when wandering reenactors allow you to debate the rights of man with Thomas Jefferson or gossip with Martha Washington about her husband's snoring.

Theater, Music, and Other Nightlife

J. M. Randall's Restaurant and Lounge (4854 Longhill Rd. in the Olde Towne Square, 757/259-0406) features acoustic rock and blues. **The Corner Pocket** (4805 Courthouse

COAST AREA WINERIES

Belle Mount Vineyards
2570 Newland Rd., Warsaw
804/333-4700
www.bellemount.com

Bloxom Vineyards
26130 Mason Rd., Bloxom
757/665-5670
www.bloxomwinery.com

Ingleside Plantation Vineyards
5872 Leedstown Rd., Oak Grove
804/224-8687
www.inglesidevineyards.com

James River Cellars
11008 Washington Hwy., Glen Allen
804/550-7516
www.jamesrivercellars.com

Lake Anna Winery
5621 Courthouse Rd., Spotsylvania
540/895-5085
www.lawinery.com

Oak Crest Vineyard & Winery
8215 Oak Crest Dr., King George
540/663-2813
www.oakcrestwinery.com

Williamsburg Winery
5800 Wessex Hundred, Williamsburg
757/229-0999
www.williamsburgwinery.com

foreign and indie films, classic cinema, and documentaries, making it a popular choice with William and Mary students and faculty. In fact, the college's Global Film Festival is held here in mid-February. The Kimball also has a 35-seat screening room on the 2nd floor. Tickets ($7) can be purchased at the box office (open 4–9 P.M. daily) or any Colonial Williamsburg ticket location. See the website for current programming.

The Williamsburg Players (200 Hubbard Ln., 757/229-0431, www.williamsburgplayers .org) is the city's oldest continuously operating community theater, in operation since 1957. Performances are held in an intimate venue where you're never far from the stage.

Outdoor Recreation

You can rent bicycles from **Bikes Unlimited** (141 Monticello Ave., 757/229-4620), which sponsors William and Mary's cycling team. Comfort bikes with big cushy seats cost $20/day, and road and mountain bikes go for $40/day.

Tours

The darker side of Williamsburg's history is the focus of the **Ghosts of Williamsburg Tours** (757/253-1058 or 877/624-4678, www.the ghosttour.com). Historical interpreters lead candlelit tours of town, weaving tales of history, ghosts, and other interesting tidbits. Tours ($11 pp age 7 and up) leave nightly at 8 P.M. and also at 8:45 P.M. June–August.

SHOPPING

Williamsburg has droves of shops, so the trick is figuring out what you want to buy, not where to buy it. Outlets galore fill malls and shopping centers in every direction from the historic center, but the most distinctive souvenirs come from specialty shops in and around Colonial Williamsburg.

Most of the items you can see being made by Williamsburg craftspeople are for sale in several **craft houses** run by the Colonial Williamsburg Foundation in Merchants Square, which is also home to various upscale shops. **The Peanut Shop** (414 Prince George

St., 757/220-0808), in the Williamsburg Crossing Shopping Center at Routes 5 and 199, is an upscale 18-and-over pool hall with high-quality tables and occasional live music.

The coziest place to see a movie in town is the **Kimball Theatre** (428 Duke of Gloucester, 757/565-8588 or 800/447-8679, www.kimball theatre.com). Even though it's right smack in the center of Colonial Williamsburg (in Merchants Square), the 410-seat theater is far from traditional. This is the go-to venue for

St., 757/229-3908) has dozens of sweet and salty snacks to sample, and there's plenty to peruse in **The Toymaker of Williamsburg** (415 Duke of Gloucester St., 757/229-5660) and the **Shirley Pewter Shop** (417 Duke of Gloucester St., 757/229-5356) next door. For something different, head to **Mermaid Books** (421-A Prince George St., 757/229-3603), a hole-in-the-wall new-and-used bookseller under Smithfield Ham Shoppe that, besides stacks of literature, sells vintage crockery and quirky mermaid paraphernalia. The **Williamsburg Farmers Market** (www.williamsburgfarmers market.com) is a real charmer too. It sets up in Merchants Square 8 A.M.–noon on Saturdays year-round, as well as 10 A.M.–2 P.M. Tuesdays in June–August.

Farther afield, **Williamsburg Pottery** (6692 Richmond Rd., 757/564-3326, www.williams burgpottery.com) has grown so large since it opened in 1938 that it now has its own campground. It's been called "the greatest assemblage of kitsch in America," with items from over 20 countries.

EVENTS

In early October, the **Williamsburg Scottish Festival and Celtic Celebration** (www .wsfonline.org) brings bagpipes, brogues, and a Balmoral reception to the Rockahock Campgrounds (www.rockahock.com). Celtic dancing, clan tents, and a ceilidh (Scottish musical party) round out the festivities.

The Christmas holiday season is one of Colonial Williamsburg's busiest times, beginning with the **Grand Illumination** in early December, when the entire historic area flickers with candlelight. Homes are hung with natural decorations such as pinecones and evergreen boughs, and the streets echo with concerts and carols. Special holiday programs, concerts, feasts, fireworks, and military salutes continue through New Year's Eve, when there's a **First Night** celebration.

ACCOMMODATIONS

With more than 10,000 hotel rooms, Williamsburg has no shortage of places to stay. Still, this is such a popular destination that reservations are always helpful—and essential during the peak periods of April, May, July, August, October, late November, and December.

Colonial Williamsburg Foundation Hotels

For information and reservations for these accommodations in the historic area, contact the Colonial Williamsburg Foundation (800/447-8679, www.history.org).

What could be more authentic after a long day in the 18th century than curling up in an actual Colonial home? The foundation operates 26 **Colonial houses**, each with its own unique history and anywhere from one to 16 rooms. The **Market Square Tavern** is where Thomas Jefferson lodged as a student at William and Mary; the **Quarter** was a favorite of Cary Grant in the 1940s. Some of the buildings, including the **Bracken Tenement** and **Ewing House,** are original, whereas others are reconstructed. Many have canopied beds, fireplaces, period antiques, and views of Duke of Gloucester Street. Prices range $150–460; see the foundation's website for details and reservations.

The **C Williamsburg Inn** (136 E. Francis St., 757/253-2277) is probably the finest hotel in the city, if not the entire Historic Peninsula. Renovations completed in 2001 enlarged the hotel to 62 rooms and upped its AAA category to four diamonds. No two rooms in this posh place are alike, but all are lavishly decorated with antiques. The inn's formal Regency Dining Room is justly famous for its elegant setting and extensive wine list; the Regency Lounge provides a more casual option. English tea is served several days a week. Guests have access to full sports facilities and three golf courses, including the nationally known Golden Horseshoe. Rates are $300 and up.

The **Williamsburg Lodge** (310 S. England St., 757/220-7976) is a resort hotel popular with conference groups. Three hundred rooms and 24 suites alternate between Colonial and modern decor, and the sunken garden is perfect for an after-dinner ramble. Dining choices include the Bay Room Restaurant and the relaxed Lodge Cafe. Prices start at around $130.

The **Woodlands Hotel** (105 Visitors Center Dr., 757/220-7690) offers 204 contemporary rooms and 96 suites in comfortably wooded surroundings next door to the Colonial Williamsburg visitors center. It's one of the foundation's less expensive lodging options, with rooms for $70–160.

The **Governor's Inn** (506 N. Henry St., 757/220-7940, $60–100) began its career as a Sheraton a short walk from the visitors center and the historic area. It has 200 rooms and a pool that's open seasonally. The Governor's Inn is usually closed January–mid-March.

$50-100

The **White Lion Motel** (912 Capitol Landing Rd., 757/229-3931, www.whitelionmotel.com) has rooms for $52–78 and efficiency suites for up to $100. The **Days Inn Historic Area** (331 Bypass Rd., 757/253-1166, $70–100) goes for a country-inn atmosphere in its 120 rooms, including some suites. Two other inexpensive lodging options near the historic area are the **Quarterpath Inn** (620 York St., 757/220-0960, www.quarterpathinn.com, $55–100) and the **Econo Lodge** (216 Parkway Dr., 757/253-6450, $55–90).

$100-150

German-born Inge Curtis opened **Primrose Cottage at Two Rivers** (16538 Chickahominy Bluff Rd., 800/522-1901, www.primrose-cottage.com, $195) as an outlet for her interests in cooking, gardening, and carpentry, and it shows in the beds of pansies and primroses in the front yard.

The **Colonial Capital Bed & Breakfast** (501 Richmond Rd., 757/229-0233 or 800/776-0570, www.ccbb.com, $145–160) occupies a 1926 Colonial Revival home across the street from the College of William and Mary. Oriental rugs and family heirlooms fill the three-story house, whose large plantation parlor is warmed by a roaring fire in the winter.

$150-200

At the **Colonial Gardens Bed & Breakfast** (1109 Jamestown Rd., 800/886-9715, www.colonial-gardens.com, $155–185), rocking chairs sit on the front porch and plush robes wait in the bedrooms, named after the rhododendrons and azaleas that bloom in the gardens. Breakfast is served on fine china in the formal dining room, and over the holidays a Christmas tree brightens each room.

The **(Newport House B&B** (710 S. Henry St., 757/229-1775 or 877/565-1775, www.newporthousebb.com, $150–225) is Williamsburg's most historically themed bed-and-breakfast. It's a 1998 museum-standard reconstruction of a 1756 home designed by Colonial architect Peter Harrison, with wood siding carved to look like cut stone (Harrison's solution for a client who couldn't afford a stone house). The two rooms are furnished with top-notch English and American antiques, accurate down to the bedspread patterns. Hosts John and Cathy Millar teach English country dancing in the ballroom and often include a historic recipe or two for breakfast. Josephine Bunnyparts is the resident rabbit.

Over $200

Century-old beech, oak, and poplar trees welcome you to the **(Liberty Rose B&B** (1025 Jamestown Rd., 757/253-1260 or 800/545-1825, www.libertyrose.com, $195–245), called the most romantic bed-and-breakfast in Williamsburg. Set on a hilltop, the two-story home features rooms with names like Magnolias Peach and Savannah Lace, decorated with designer wall coverings and vintage fabrics. Soak in an antique claw-foot tub or savor a gourmet breakfast on the sunny porch.

Five miles east of Colonial Williamsburg on U.S. 60 is **Kingsmill Resort** (757/253-1703 or 800/832-5665, www.kingsmill.com), the state's largest golf and spa resort. Three 18-hole championship golf courses on the banks of the James River include the difficult River Course, site of the Michelob Championship at Kingsmill for 22 years and currently part of the LPGA tour. Fifteen tennis courts, a marina, nature trails, and a full fitness center–spa round out the amenities, and there are six restaurants and lounges to choose from for meals. More than 400 guest rooms and suites with 1–3 bedrooms and kitchens cost from $170 upward. Call for information on various package deals, including admission to Colonial Williamsburg and nearby attractions.

Camping

The **Anvil Campground** (5243 Mooretown Rd., 757/565-2300 or 800/633-4442, www .anvilcampground.com, open year-round) is the closest to central Williamsburg. A laundry, TV room, three playgrounds, and basketball courts are just some of the services offered. Sites are $35–50, and there are cottages for $120–130.

Take Route 646 north from I-64 exit 234 (Lightfoot) to reach the **Williamsburg KOA Resort** (4000 Newman Rd., 800/562-1733, www.williamsburgkoa.com, open Mar.–Dec.), a hefty 180-acre 370-site campground. Campsites ($35–58) and one- and two-room cabins ($60–90) are available.

FOOD
Snacks and Cafés

Savor the smells of **Aromas** (431 Prince George St., 757/221-6676, all meals daily), a coffeehouse and then some where you can find gourmet coffees and teas along with smoothies, fresh pastries, sandwiches, and a full breakfast and dinner menu. Wine and beer are also on the menu, and live music happens on weekend nights. More excellent coffee drinks await at **The Coffeehouse** (5251-6 John Tyler Hwy., 757/229-9791, breakfast and lunch daily) in the Williamsburg Crossing Shopping Center. Sandwiches, muffins, and bagels from scratch round things out, and there's an outdoor terrace for sunny weather. Both are good meeting places—or refuges from historic overload.

Casual

Half restaurant, half antiques shop, the **Old Chickahominy House** (1211 Jamestown Rd., 757/229-4689, breakfast and lunch daily) resembles an old farmhouse and serves food to match. Plantation meals in the 18th-century dining room include chicken and dumplings and homemade pie; hearty country breakfasts of Virginia ham, bacon, sausage, eggs, grits, and biscuits are around $7–8. (The pancakes are excellent.)

Inexpensive pizzas, subs, sandwiches, and steamed seafood are the standard favorites at **The Library Tavern** (1330 Richmond Rd., 757/229-1012, lunch and dinner daily, open until 2 A.M., $7–16), "where silence isn't golden." There's a full bar and pool tables in the back.

For a greasy-spoon diner with a friendly waitstaff, you can't beat **(Five Forks Café** (4456 John Tyler Hwy., 757/221-0484, all meals Tues.–Sat., breakfast and lunch Sun.). At breakfast, mix and match fillings for a three-egg omelet, or fill up on blueberry pancakes or biscuits and gravy. For dinner, the most expensive item on the menu is also the most traditional: roasted turkey with cranberry sauce for $11. Active duty military get a 25 percent discount with their military identification card.

(The Cheese Shop (410 Duke of Gloucester St., 757/220-0298, 10 A.M.–9 P.M. Mon.–Sat., 11 A.M.–6 P.M. Sun.) offers over 200 types of cheese (and samples!) along with fresh-baked bread, sandwiches, and a wine cellar with thousands of bottles on offer. It's next to Fat Canary on Merchant Square and run by the same folks.

Fresh seafood is the specialty, naturally, of **The Whaling Company** (494 McLaws Circle, 757/229-0275, dinner daily), on Route 60 East near Busch Gardens. Plates like shrimp scampi linguine run $13–38, and the hand-carved steaks are also worth a mention.

Take a lunch stop at the **Jamestown Pie Company** (1804 Jamestown Rd., 757/229-7775, lunch and dinner daily), where "round food is good food"—namely pizzas ($15–23 for a 16-inch), pot pies ($9–11 individual pie), and dessert pies ($14–18). This pizzeria and pie company is a convenient stop en route to Jamestown from Williamsburg on Route 31. It's take-out only, but there are a few tables on the patio.

Upscale

Billing itself as "serious comfort food," the **(** **Blue Talon Bistro** (420 Prince George St., 757/476-2583, all meals daily) dresses up classics like mac-and-cheese and meatloaf in their Sunday best ($16–26). Check out the plate of the day for specials such as shrimp and polenta or braised goat with a yellow curry sauce. Blue Talon is located on the perimeter of Merchants Square in Colonial Williamsburg. You can watch the chefs in their starched white jackets and hats whipping up delicious entrées from a window on the sidewalk along Prince George Street.

The confections of original owner Marcel Desaulniers, author of the popular dessert manual *Death by Chocolate,* are reason enough to visit **The Trellis Restaurant** (403 Duke of Gloucester St., 757/229-8610, lunch and dinner daily). In early 2010, the Trellis came under the wing of Blue Talon Bistro's management and underwent a $1 million renovation. After choosing a new look and a new menu for the Trellis emphasizing local cuisine such as rockfish and pan-roasted chicken and Virginia wines, new executive chef David Everett has left one thing unchanged: Desserts continue to be lethal. While Desaulniers is no longer in the kitchen, many of his original recipes endure.

Overlooking Merchants Square is **(** **Fat Canary** (410 Duke of Gloucester St., 757/229-3333, dinner daily), a modern gourmet dining room with an open kitchen and a stylish bar. The food is pricey but fantastic—Fat Canary has earned the prestigious AAA Four Diamond award every year since it opened in 2003 (at least as of 2010). Chef Thomas Power draws on the seasons for the freshest ingredients, concocting plates such as pan-seared monkfish with lemon and fennel risotto for $26–38.

Historic Dining

Colonial Williamsburg's four reconstructed taverns carry on the tradition of "savory victuals." Low-beamed ceilings, roaring fireplaces, and pewter plates evoke the days when wealthy planters gathered to dine on classic dishes such as peanut soup, Sally Lund bread, and Brunswick stew. All of the taverns have garden seating in cooperative weather, and some have roving balladeers and costumed servers. Reservations are required (757/229-2141) unless noted otherwise, and most of these establishments operate seasonally (Apr.–Dec.).

Christiana Campbell's Tavern (101 S. Waller St., dinner daily, Tues.–Sat. off-season) specializes in seafood; Mrs. Campbell's gumbo and Carolina fish muddle were favorites of George Washington ($20–34).

Grilled poultry, seafood, and Colonial game pie are served in candlelit elegance at the **King's Arms Tavern** (416 E. Duke of Gloucester St., lunch and dinner daily). Top it off with a slice of pecan pie and goblet of Colonial punch. Lunch entrées such as fried chicken and sandwiches cost $12–14; dinner entrées cost $27–34.

The **(** **Shields Tavern** (422 E. Duke of Gloucester St., lunch and dinner daily) next door is the oldest and largest tavern in Williamsburg, re-creating a rustic eatery of the late 1740s. Eleven dining rooms fill with the smell of pork chops baking and beef roasting on a specially designed spit. Other tempting choices, including the catch of the day and filet mignon (around $25), go well with a mug of sparkling cider.

Adjacent to the Courthouse is **Josiah Chowning's Tavern** (109 E. Duke of Gloucester St., lunch and dinner daily), opened in 1766. Mr. Chowning's black walnut ice cream is a standout after a heaping plateful of baked stuffed pork chops. After 9 P.M., you can knock back a tankard or two in a setting rich with 18th-century music and games in Gambol's pub. Reservations are not required here.

INFORMATION

The best sources of information are the **Colonial Williamsburg Foundation** (800/447-8679, www.history.org) and the **Greater Williamsburg Area Chamber & Tourism Alliance** (421 N. Boundary St., 757/229-6511 or 800/368-6511, www.williamsburgcc.com).

GETTING THERE AND AROUND
Getting There

The **Williamsburg Transportation Center** (468 N. Boundary St. at Lafayette) houses the terminals of Greyhound (757/229-1460) and Amtrak (757/229-8750). Here you can also catch a ride with Yellow Cab of Williamsburg (757/722-1111).

Fourteen miles east of Williamsburg, at I-64 exit 255 in Newport News, is the **Newport News-Williamsburg International Airport** (900 Bland Blvd., 757/877-0221, www.nnw airport.com), served by AirTran, U.S. Airways Express, Frontier, and Delta Connections. Both the transportation center and the airport have a handful of car rental agencies.

Getting Around

Public buses are managed by **Williamsburg Area Transport** (757/220-5493 or 757/259-4093, www.williamsburgtransport.com). Buses ($1.25–1.50 one way, exact fare required) run 6 A.M.–8 or 10 P.M. Monday–Saturday, 8 A.M.–5 P.M. Sunday. Call or see the website for routes and times.

The same agency operates the jaunty red-and-green **Williamsburg Trolley** on a loop around Merchants Square, the Williamsburg Shopping Center, High Street, and New Town. Rides cost $0.50 (exact change required) and the trolley runs 3–10 P.M. Monday–Thursday, 3–11 P.M. Saturday, and noon–8 P.M. Sunday.

Colonial Williamsburg's own **shuttle buses** are the easiest way to get around the historic area, stopping at the visitors center, Merchants Square, the Magazine, Governor's Palace, and capitol building.

NEAR WILLIAMSBURG
York River State Park

A rugged landscape of gorge, forest, marsh, and bluff covers 2,500 brackish acres where Taskinas Creek meets the York River. The site of public tobacco warehouses in the 17th and 18th centuries, when it was known as Taskinas Plantation, this park has a much longer history than that: Fossilized whale vertebrae, sharks' teeth, and coral up to five million years old have all been found nearby.

More than 25 miles of trails connect the river, creek, and freshwater ponds plied by anglers during fishing season (boat rentals are available). Guided canoe trips—including moonlight trips—up the tidal waters of Taskinas Creek (May–Oct.) leave from the **Taskinas Point Visitors Center** (757/566-3036, www.dcr.virginia.gov/state_parks/yor .shtml, $3), and interpretive programs explore the park's fossils and natural offerings. The visitors center is off I-64 exit 231 to Route 507 north; continue to Route 606; within one mile, take a right, continue 1.5 miles, and take a left onto Route 696.

Busch Gardens Europe

Historic recreation takes on a slightly different meaning in Virginia's largest amusement park, repeatedly voted America's most beautiful for its Old World theme. Roller coasters are the stars, beginning with Griffon, the world's tallest and first "floorless dive coaster," which hauls riders 205 feet before sending them down the track at 75 mph. On the Alpengeist, passengers hang from the track as if on a ski lift, although the similarity ends when the ride hits 3.7 Gs during the "cobra roll."

Get an up-close look at the gray wolves at Jack Hanna's Wild Reserve or Big Bird and Elmo from *Sesame Street,* and you won't believe how big and beautiful the Clydesdales in the Highland Stables are. If you get hungry (tip: wait until *after* you ride the Alpengeist), you'll find wurst, beer, and an oompah band in the 2,000-seat Festhaus.

Busch Gardens (800/343-7946, www .buschgardens.com, $62 adults, $52 children, $12 parking, opens 10 A.M. daily June–Aug., weekends only Apr.–May, Sept.–Oct., and Dec., closing hours vary) is off U.S. 60 three miles southeast of Williamsburg. Various family packages are available.

Water Country USA

Busch Gardens' sister park is the mid-Atlantic's largest water park, which offers more than 30 ways to escape the summer swelter. Splash through the darkened tunnels of the Aquazoid; team up for the Meltdown, a three-person water toboggan; or hit escape velocity on the super-speed 320-foot Nitro Racer water-slide. The H2O UFO and Cow-a-Bunga areas are geared toward kids, and whole families can enjoy the wave pools and dive shows.

Water Country USA (800/343-7946, www .watercountryusa.com, $43 adults, $36 children 3–9, $12 parking, opens 10 A.M. daily Memorial Day–Labor Day, closing times vary) is on Water Country Parkway (Rte. 199) near Busch Gardens.

JAMESTOWN

The first "successful" permanent English colony in America began as James Fort, hastily erected in 1607 by a handful of nervous settlers who had traded three cramped sailboats for an endless, untamed wilderness. A combination of sickness, inexperience, hostile natives, and bad management almost spelled the colony's doom in the first few years, but the leadership of Capt. John Smith and a series of fragile truces with the local tribes allowed 5,000 inhabitants to survive to 1634.

It all fell to ruins after the Colonial capital was moved to Williamsburg in 1699. A Confederate fort took the place of the original wooden stockade in 1861, a year before Jamestown Island was occupied by Union troops. In 1933, the island became part of the Colonial National Historical Park. In the late 1980s, an archaeological reassessment led to the discovery of the original settlement (part of which had been hidden by the shifting currents of the James River). Further excavations uncovered the triangular footprint of the Jamestown fort in 1994.

Two separate locations provide contrasting interpretations of the site. First comes Jamestown Settlement, a re-creation of life on the pitiless frontier run by the Commonwealth of Virginia. Across the bridge is the real thing, on Jamestown Island, a much more low-key but equally affecting spot maintained by the National Park Service. In both locations, major

enhancements coincided with the celebrations in 2007 of the 400th anniversary of the settlers' landing.

Jamestown Settlement

Hardy colonists and their native counterparts come to life in this living-history museum of life in 17th-century Virginia—albeit a somewhat sanitized and user-friendly version—down to the smell of cooking fires and the roar of gunpowder muskets. Start at the museum, packed with artifacts and information on the English pioneers and their alternating allies and enemies, the Powhatan Indians, as well as Africans who arrived in Virginia in the 1600s. Catch the film *1607: A Nation Takes Root* before you step outside for the real attractions.

First comes the **Powhatan Indian village,** half a dozen domed houses made of woven reeds over sapling frames. Here, interpreters costumed in animal skins show you how to make stone and bone tools, scrape hides, and weave plant fibers into cordage. Kids will enjoy grinding corn (at least for a while) and will probably ask about the ceremonial circle of wooden poles carved with faces.

A short walk down the path brings you to the river pier, where three life-size **ship reproductions** of the vessels that brought the European settlers are tied up. Cormorants fish in the water next to the *Discovery,* the *Godspeed,* and the *Susan Constant.* Climb aboard and imagine crossing 6,000 miles of open ocean in quarters this cramped—the smallest craft is only 66 feet long, with roughly as much space as a school bus. The *Susan Constant,* the largest, is 116 feet long with a brightly painted hull. Reenactors will point out the brick hearth (surprising on a wooden ship) and demonstrate various shipboard activities, including furling sails and handling cargo. These are fully functioning ships, and they occasionally sail away to participate in nautical events.

The colonists must have breathed a sigh of relief to step out into the safety and relative spaciousness of **James Fort,** which has been carefully re-created as it was in 1610–1614. Tall wooden palisades connect three raised circular

COURTESY JAMESTOWN-YORKTOWN FOUNDATION

Reproductions of the 1607 English ships – *Godspeed, Discovery,* and *Susan Constant* – are moored at Jamestown Settlement's pier.

platforms at each corner. Farm fields stretch beyond the walls, while inside stand wattle-and-daub homes, a church, a guardhouse, and storehouses. Try your hand at ninepins (an early version of bowling), and cover your ears for the periodic firing of matchlock muskets.

Yearly events start in mid-March with **Military through the Ages,** with reenactors demonstrating weapons, tactics, and camp life; **Jamestown Landing Day** in mid-May brings more living-history demonstrations. **Virginia Indian Heritage Day** in June celebrates the importance of the Powhatan Indians, complete with drumming and dancing from multiple tribes in the region. In late November, Jamestown hosts **Foods & Feasts of Colonial Virginia,** a three-day Thanksgiving event focusing on Colonial and native food, followed by **A Colonial Christmas,** showcasing 17th- and 18th-century holiday decorations and traditional activities.

Jamestown Settlement (9 A.M.–5 P.M. daily, until 6 P.M. mid-June–mid-Aug., $14 adults, $6.50 children 6–12) has a gift shop and café and is managed by the **Jamestown-Yorktown Foundation** (757/253-4838 or 888/593-4682, www.historyisfun.org). A combination ticket including the Yorktown Victory Center is available for $19.25 adults, $9.25 children.

Jamestown Island (Colonial National Historical Park)

The earlier end of this elongated park begins with the **Jamestown Glasshouse of 1608,** next to the ruins of the original brick and riverstone furnaces. The first factory industry in the colonies folded after one shipment to England, but artisans in the reconstructed workshop still sell lovely handblown glassware made from the same mixture of ash and sand.

Keep driving across a narrow spit of land into the island to reach the National Park Service **visitors center,** which shows an 18-minute orientation video. You can explore Olde Towne and New Towne on your own or join the ranger-led walks. Part of the original town

© KATIE GITHENS

English colonists hastily built James Fort to protect against the Spanish, who never attacked.

site has been inundated as the James River shoreline shifted, but brick outlines mark where certain buildings once stood. The oldest standing structure is the 1639 tower of the Memorial Church, near statues of Pocahontas and Capt. John Smith. A memorial cross marks 300 shallow graves dug during the Starving Time of 1609–1610. Standing on the edge of the windswept beach with the sparse logs of the reconstructed fort behind you, life as a colonist suddenly seems startlingly real—and lonesome.

Queen Elizabeth II showed up for Jamestown's 400th anniversary celebrations in 2007, which heralded a number of improvements to this part of the park, including a monument commemorating the four centuries since the English arrived and a café (open seasonally). A glass-walled "archaerium" now displays archaeological findings, and virtual viewers let you see what things looked like four centuries ago using computerized videos. This museum houses one of the largest collections of 17th-century artifacts in the country. Everyday

utensils including hairpins, buckles, and candlesticks invoke the real people who suffered, survived, and died on this swampy island an ocean away from anything safe and familiar.

Along the five-mile wilderness loop drive, which can be shortened to three, you'll stand a good chance of spotting descendants of the same deer, muskrats, and water birds hunted by the Jamestown settlers.

Living-history programs and children's activities are held in June and July. Annual events include **Jamestown Day,** celebrating the founding of the colony, in mid-May; the **First Assembly Day Commemoration** in late July; **Arrival of the First Africans,** examining slavery's start in Jamestown and the contributions of early African Americans in Virginia in mid-August; and an evening walking tour and symbolic torching of the town in late September near the anniversary of **Bacon's Rebellion** in 1676.

Admission to Jamestown Island (757/229-1733, www.nps.gov/jame, 9 A.M.–5 P.M. daily, $10 adults, free for children 15 and

© KATIE GITHENS

During the "Starving Time," the winter of 1609-1610, only 60 of the 400-500 settlers living at Jamestown survived.

under) is good for a week and includes the Yorktown Battlefield. For more information on the archaeological angle, see the website of Preservation Virginia's Jamestown Rediscovery project (www.historicjamestowne.org).

YORKTOWN

One of Virginia's major ports in the 18th century, Yorktown rivaled Williamsburg with its thriving waterfront at the base of a bluff beneath Main Street's regal homes. Almost 2,000 people lived here when Lord Cornwallis arrived in 1781, pursued by the American army and the French navy just offshore during the Revolutionary War. Days of bombardment convinced the British general to request a meeting on October 17 and to surrender officially two days later. The 225th anniversary of the battle was celebrated in 2006.

Yorktown Visitors Center (Colonial National Historical Park)

The earth ramparts erected by George Washington's troops now defend this museum,

filled with various relics saved from the final confrontation of the Revolutionary War. George Washington's field tents are displayed next to surrendered flags and a rifle stock broken by a British soldier in disgust. Walk through a partial reconstruction of a British warship (watch your head), and get your bearings through a narrated map presentation.

Walking tours, led by rangers or interpreters in costume and character, leave from here for the British Inner Defensive Line and the town of Yorktown, exploring Surrender Field, George Washington's headquarters, and earthworks reconstructed through archaeological excavations and detailed studies of 18th-century military maps.

Like Jamestown Island, the Yorktown Visitors Center (757/898-2410, www.nps.gov/colo, 9 A.M.–5 P.M. daily, $10) is administered by the National Park Service. Tickets are good for a week and include admission to Jamestown Island as well. A free trolley runs down into town and back every half hour or so during summer.

Yorktown Victory Center

This well-done museum and living-history center sits across U.S. 17 from Yorktown. Brush up on your background knowledge along the outdoor timeline that leads inside the main building, where exhibits on people affected by the war—from slaves to common women to soldiers—are told through narrated recordings, films, relics, and documents. Don't miss the Declaration of Independence on display; it's a rare broadside printing that dates back to July 18, 1776—not the original handwritten parchment version signed by members of Congress that's today on display at the National Archives in Washington, D.C., but nearly as old.

Outside, at the Continental Army encampment, you can try on a soldier's coat, learn about medicine, food, and music in Colonial armies, and become one of the 17 people needed to fire a cannon (unloaded, of course). A short distance away is a reconstructed farm site typical of a lower- to middle-class family of the late 18th century. A tobacco barn, kitchen building, and modest home stand next to vegetable and herb gardens and animal pens, managed by costumed interpreters who demonstrate Colonial cooking, farming, and games.

The center (9 A.M.–5 P.M. daily, until 6 P.M. mid-June–mid-Aug., $9.50 adults, $5.25 children 6–12) operates under the auspices of the state-run **Jamestown-Yorktown Foundation** (757/253-4838 or 888/593-4682, www.history isfun.org). A combination ticket including the Jamestown Settlement is available for $19.25 adults, $9.25 children. There's also a large gift shop with a beverage and snack vending area.

As you can imagine, the Fourth of July is a big deal around here, and it's saluted with the **Liberty Celebration,** a blitz of 18th-century military drills and reenactments to honor America's independence. More skirmishes with Redcoats fire away in October during the **Yorktown Victory Celebration,** commemorating the game-changing Revolutionary War victory on October 19, 1781. Holiday celebrations for Thanksgiving and Christmas also find their way into the Yorktown Victory Center's educational programming.

A rare broadside printing of the Declaration of Independence is on display at the Yorktown Victory Center.

COURTESY JAMESTOWN-YORKTOWN FOUNDATION

Historic Yorktown

Still a sparse but working village, Yorktown counts dozens of homes more than two centuries old, many of which occupy their own "lots" (blocks) on the fringes. A path from the visitors center takes you past the 84-foot **Victory Monument,** topped by a winged statue of Liberty, to **Cornwallis's Cave** on the riverbank, a dank hole where the British general is said to have made his headquarters during the shelling. The **Nelson House** was once home to Thomas Nelson Jr., a signer of the Declaration of Independence. It still bears scars from cannonballs directed by Nelson, who suspected Cornwallis was inside. The terms of surrender were drafted in the **Moore House.**

Yorktown's military past tends to be what's on display. **Civil War Weekend** in late May observes Memorial Day and includes musical performances on the waterfront. In mid-October, Yorktown's better-known **Revolutionary War** weekend features fife and drum players on parade, encampments, and demonstrations.

History of a different sort is remembered in the **Watermen's Museum** (309 Water St., 757/887-2641, www.watermens.org, 10 A.M.–5 P.M. Tues.–Sat., 1–5 P.M. Sun. in season, weekends only Thanksgiving–Mar., $3). Boat models, marine life, and a boat-building area out back honor the "iron men and wooden boats" who have fished the local waters since the first Indians ventured out in dugout canoes. A gift shop sells work by local artists. It's near the U.S. 17 bridge by the water.

Activities

The Colonial-themed **Riverwalk Landing** development (www.riverwalklanding.com) features a year-round performance area, a beach, two floating piers, and a mile-long pedestrian walkway by the York River. Sail aboard the 105-foot schooner *Alliance* (757/639-1233, www.schooneralliance.com), home ported in Yorktown from May through October (and in the Caribbean the rest of the year). Daily sails leave from Riverwalk Landing at 11 A.M. and 2 P.M. (May–Oct., $30 adults, $18 children), and sunset sails (call for departure times) are $35 per person. Try to buy tickets online ahead of time; both the daily sails and the sunset sails sell out.

Accommodations and Food

The **Duke of York Hotel** (508 Water St., 757/898-3232, www.dukeofyorkmotel.com, $75–180) offers beachfront and river-view rooms as well as an outdoor pool. Set on a high bluff above the Watermen's Museum, the **York River Inn** (209 Ambler St., 757/887-8800 or 800/884-7003, www.yorkriverinn.com) is an elegant little bed-and-breakfast with two rooms and a suite ($115–140). The **Marl Inn Bed & Breakfast** (220 Church St., 757/898-3859, www.marlinnbandb.com, $110 d, $130–150 suite) is only a few blocks away—but then again, so is everything in this tiny town.

You can grab a bite along the water at the **Yorktown Pub** (112 Water St., 757/886-9964, lunch and dinner daily, $5–11 lunch, $19–22

dinner), with hearty food, homemade desserts, and live music on weekend nights. It accepts cash only.

The Dining Room at **Nick's Riverwalk Restaurant** (323 Water St., 757/875-1522, lunch and dinner daily) is one of the more upscale places to eat along the Riverwalk Landing strip, with seafood-centric main dishes such as Chesapeake stew or seared scallops wrapped in prosciutto ($11–15 lunch, $17–30 dinner). Sandwiches, salads, and pizzas are also served on the sunny patio of the restaurant's more casual **Rivah Café**.

The ◖ **Carrot Tree** (411 Main St., 757/988-1999, lunch daily, dinner Thurs.–Sat.) in the Cole Digges House, Yorktown's oldest home, features soups, salads, and sandwiches from scratch ($6–14)—and a carrot cake you'll wish could grow on trees. High tea is served at 4 P.M. on Wednesdays, often with a literary theme and readings. Dinner turns more savory, with stuffed pork tenderloin, tomato tarts, and Battlefield Beef Stroganoff ($14–15). There's a kids menu with familiar favorites like PB&J.

Information

Find information on the town and its environs in **The Gallery at York Hall** (Main and Ballard Sts., 757/890-4490, 10 A.M.–4 P.M. Tues.–Sat., 1–4 P.M. Sun., open seasonally Apr.–Dec.). Otherwise contact Historic Yorktown at 757/890-3500, www.yorkcounty.gov/tourism.

◖ JAMES RIVER PLANTATIONS

The fertile banks of the lower James have been prime real estate ever since the days of the Powhatan capital at Sandy Point. During the 18th and 19th centuries, lavish mansions served as business and social centers for huge tobacco plantations. Carriages no longer clatter down long, tree-shaded gravel lanes, with servants waiting to escort visitors into the parlor for tea and talk of planting, but the area is still mostly forest and farmland with no major town center. (There is no city in Charles City County.)

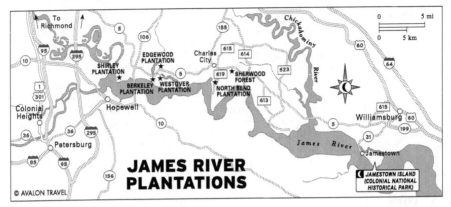

Route 5, also called the John Tyler Highway, leads straight from Richmond to six major plantations along the river's north bank. Annual events such as garden tours, special teas, birthday celebrations, and progressive luncheons happen almost every month of the year. Best of all, the drive is gorgeous. If you're traveling between Richmond and the Historic Peninsula, skip I-64 and its pell-mell traffic and take to this leafy country byway instead. It adds very little driving time and is worth the peace of mind.

Shirley Plantation

Virginia's oldest plantation sits on land settled in 1613 by Sir Thomas West. Begun in 1723 and finished in 1738, the house survived both the Revolutionary and Civil Wars and is the

Berkeley Plantation

birthplace of Anne Hill Carter Lee, mother of Robert E., who married Light-Horse Harry in the parlor. Today, Shirley Plantation (804/829-5121 or 800/232-1613, www.shirleyplantation .com, 9:30 A.M.–4:30 P.M. daily, $11 adults, $7.50 children 6–18) is home to the 11th and 12th generations of the Hill-Carter family, plenty of heirlooms, and centuries of stories. Guided house tours run throughout the day.

Berkeley Plantation

On December 4, 1619, 38 English settlers kissed the earth and thanked the heavens upon landing partway up the James River after three months at sea. A monument marks the spot where many scholars believe the first Thanksgiving took place—followed two years later by the first batch of bourbon whiskey distilled in the New World. While the Thanksgiving memorial—an understated stone arch on the banks of the James—is anticlimactic, it's a peaceful spot and the plantation has its own charms.

The Harrison family bought this property in 1691. Benjamin Harrison IV built the manor house in 1726, leaving a stone bearing the date and his and his wife's initials over a side door. His son Benjamin V signed the Declaration of Independence and served three terms as governor of Virginia. *His* son William Henry became the ninth president of the United States after making his name on the western frontier. George Washington stopped by from time to time, the first in a string of 10 presidents to enjoy the Harrisons' hospitality. Although he didn't live at Berkeley, William Henry's grandson Benjamin Harrison did the family name proud yet again by becoming the 23rd president of the United States.

During Union occupation in 1862, Gen. Dan Butterfield composed the haunting melody of "Taps" here shortly before Lincoln visited to review McClellan's army. In the 20th century, the property was lovingly restored through the efforts of Malcolm Jamieson, whose father was a Federal drummer boy. Worth a stop in themselves are Berkeley's terraced boxwood gardens, spread between the

The grounds of Berkeley Plantation witnessed the first Thanksgiving celebrated by English colonists.

house and wide lawns leading down to the river, where geese and sheep wander. The view of the James is unparalleled.

Berkeley (804/829-6018 or 888/466-6018, www.berkeleyplantation.com, 9 A.M.–5 P.M. daily, $11 adults, $7 children 13–16, $6 children 6–12) also hosts a **First Thanksgiving Festival** on the first Sunday in November, commemorating the original ceremony of gratitude with Colonial and native reenactors.

Westover Plantation

William Byrd III, founder of Richmond and Petersburg, built this Georgian manor house in the 1730s. It's famous for its elegant proportions, its view of the James, and the ancient tulip poplars around the lawn. Westover is also known as one home of the ghost of Byrd's daughter Evelyn, who pined to death at age 18 after her Catholic parents forbade her to marry a Protestant. She told friends she would come back from the beyond, and her glowing ghost has since been reported here and at Evelynton (witnesses describe it as non-threatening).

Westover (804/829-2882, www.jamesriver plantations.org/westover.html) shares an access road off Route 5 with Berkeley Plantation. The house is open only during Historic Garden Week in April, but the grounds and garden are open to visitors 9 A.M.–6 P.M. daily for $2 adults, $0.50 children.

Sherwood Forest

The only home owned by two U.S. presidents was begun in 1730 under the name Smith's Hundred. William Henry Harrison inherited it in the 1790s but never lived here, in part because he died one month after his inaugural speech. Harrison's vice president, John Tyler, took over both the presidency and ownership of this white clapboard house, where he retired in 1845. Tyler's grandson still lives upstairs.

Additions to the original building have made Sherwood Forest the longest wooden-frame house in the country at more than 300 feet. A 68-foot ballroom was designed to accommodate guests dancing the Virginia reel. Scars in the woodwork bear witness to Civil War action, and many of the furnishings and decorations belonged to President Tyler. Original outbuildings, terraced gardens, and more than 80 varieties of trees brighten the grounds. Sherwood Forest (804/829-5377, www.sherwoodforest.org, 9 A.M.–5 P.M. daily) is also home to a ghost called the Gray Lady, whose rocking has been heard in the Gray Room for more than two centuries. Access to the grounds is $10 adults, free children under 15, and admission to the house, open only by prior appointment, is $35 per person.

Accommodations and Food

Edgewood Plantation (4800 John Tyler Hwy., 804/829-2962, www.edgewoodplantation.com) hosts guests in a Gothic Revival home built in 1849 that has since served as post office, church, and Confederate signal post. Fireplaces and a two-story freestanding spiral staircase wait inside, while a 1725 gristmill, formal gardens, and pool surround the house. (Look for the "Lizzie" etched in an upstairs window by a woman who supposedly died of a broken heart waiting for her lover to return from the Civil War.) Eight guest rooms—six in the house and two in the former slaves' quarters—are $140–200.

Across Route 5 is the **North Bend Plantation** (12200 Weyanoke Rd., 804/829-5176, www.northbendplantation.com), built in 1819 for William Henry Harrison's sister Sarah. Union Gen. Philip Sheridan made his headquarters here in 1864 and dug trenches that still exist at the eastern edge of the property. The owners, the fifth generation of the Copland family to own North Bend, are happy to point out Sheridan's plantation desk, the 1914 billiard table, and a library full of rare and old books. Rates ($145–175) include a full country breakfast and use of the swimming pool.

Northern Hampton Roads

NEWPORT NEWS

Virginia's fifth-largest city (pop. 180,000), Newport News was named for Capt. Christopher Newport, pilot of the three-ship fleet that landed at Jamestown in 1607, whose "news" was word sent back to England that the settlers had arrived safely. Newport News stretches along I-64 and U.S. 60 toward the largest privately owned shipyard in the country, the massive Northrop Grumman Newport News facility.

The shipyard employs about one-tenth of the city's population, churning out nuclear attack submarines and aircraft carriers for the U.S. Navy; according to its founder's 19th-century credo: "We shall build good ships here at a profit—if we can—at a loss—if we must—but always good ships."

On their way to the largest coal-shipping port in the country, trains rattle south past one of the country's largest municipal parks and the outstanding Mariners' Museum, well worth a day's detour in itself.

◖ The Mariners' Museum

A 3,200-pound, 18-foot golden eagle figurehead ushers you into one of the best nautical collections in the world. The congressionally delegated National Maritime Museum (100 Museum Dr., 757/596-2222 or 800/581-7245, www.marinersmuseum.org, 10 A.M.–5 P.M. Wed.–Sat., noon–5 P.M. Sun., $12 adults, $7 children 6–12) displays gleaming Chris Crafts from the 1920s and 1930s, but also a handmade boat used by Cuban refugees to cross the Caribbean and an outrigger sailing canoe from Micronesia. The $30 million USS *Monitor* Center, opened with the help of the National Oceanic & Atmospheric Administration (NOAA) in 2007, draws the most fanfare. The Civil War ironclad, finally found off the coast of North Carolina in 1973, is memorialized in this state-of-the-art permanent exhibit, with two full-scale replicas, interactive displays, videos, and re-creations of the surprisingly civilized-looking officers' quarters. The original engine, turret, and propeller are on display in huge desalinization tanks.

YOU CAN'T DRIVE THE HAMPTON ROADS

Spend a little time near the mouth of the Chesapeake Bay and you'll probably start to get confused by a fair amount of the local terminology. Most important, and least distinct, is the term Hampton Roads itself.

In sea-faring lingo, "roadstead" means a safe anchorage for ships, usually in a sheltered natural harbor, which the lower Chesapeake Bay has in abundance. "Hampton" comes from the English nobleman Henry Wriothesley (RIZ-lee), the third Earl of Southampton, who financed early colonizing expeditions. What was originally the "Earl of Southampton's Roadstead," then, has been shortened over the years to "Hampton Roads."

You'll also hear Hampton Roads used to refer not only to where the James, Nansemond, and Elizabeth Rivers flow into the Chesapeake Bay, but to the entire metropolitan area surrounding it, from Newport News to Virginia Beach. Hampton Roads itself is usually divided further into the "South Side" (of the James River) – including Norfolk, Virginia Beach, Chesapeake, Portsmouth, and Suffolk – and "the Peninsula" (as in the Historic Peninsula) to the north, the setting of Newport News and Hampton itself.

Even though "Tidewater" technically refers to the entire region affected by the ebb and flow of the ocean (basically all of Virginia east of the fall line), it's often used the same way South Side is – to refer to everything south of the James River.

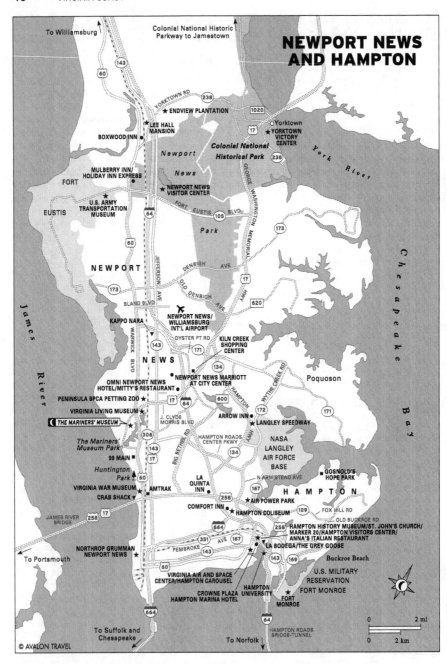

NEWPORT NEWS AND HAMPTON

© KATIE GITHENS

This hefty eagle figurehead greets you at the Mariners' Museum.

© KATIE GITHENS

At the Mariners' Museum, August and Winnifred Crabtree's miniature model ships are astonishing in their detail and beauty.

Especially remarkable are the 16 miniature model ships made over two decades by August and Winnifred Crabtree. Magnifying glasses built into the display cases let you appreciate the stunning detail, down to inch-tall figureheads carved with modified dental tools. It's a wonder the Crabtrees didn't go blind during the 20 years it took to finish the collection, which comprises everything from Indian dugouts to Columbus's ships.

You can learn how to navigate using interactive video displays in the Chesapeake Bay gallery. Other displays include knot-tying lessons, the evolution of the U.S. Navy, well-worn boat-building tools, and changing exhibits covering topics such as pirates, the slave trade, and the *Titanic.*

The same turn off U.S. 60 leads to the 550-acre **Mariners' Museum Park.** A five-mile trail circles Lake Maury, where you can rent pedalboats (757/596-2222 or 800/581-7245).

Newport News Park

Covering more than 8,000 acres, the largest city park east of the Mississippi (13560 Jefferson Ave., 757/886-7912, www.nnparks.com) is a patchwork of meadows, swamps, lakes, and hardwood forest threaded by mountain-bike, horse, and nature trails. There's an 18-hole disc golf course, a five-star archery range, and the kaleidoscopic azaleas and Japanese teahouse of the Peace Garden. Visitors can rent bikes to explore 10 miles of Civil War fortifications or take out a canoe or pedalboat to fish on Lee Hall Reservoir. The **Newport News Golf Club at Deer Run** (757/886-7925, www.nngolfclub .com) has two full courses and a driving range. You can even spend the night at one of 188 campsites (757/888-3333 or 800/203-8322), with full hookups for $28.50–31. From I-64, take exit 250B to reach the park.

Virginia Living Museum

It doesn't have statues that walk or paintings that talk, but this place does boast a bevy of wild animals in outdoor pens modeled after their natural habitats. Start in the exhibition building, where different sections of the

James River—complete with plants, catfish, and bass—have been reproduced in a series of aquariums. At the touch tank, find out why horseshoe crab blood sells for $30,000 an ounce, and try not to wake the screech owl in the World of Darkness. Many different Virginia ecosystems have been re-created here, from mountain streams to a southeastern cypress swamp.

Step outside onto the elevated boardwalk to reach open-air enclosures where raccoons scurry, bobcats pace, and otters zoom away from an underwater window in streams of bubbles. Past the raucous coastal plain aviary, home to great blue herons and snake-necked cattle egrets, are more pens containing animals native to Virginia in natural habitats. The Virginia Garden, a permanent exhibit on Virginia's botanical history from 1607 to the present, includes the native species that were present when the first settlers arrived at Jamestown and shows how Indians employed plants for food and medicine and how the colonists learned to use them in their struggle for survival.

A $22.6 million expansion added a raised outdoor aviary, housing birds from Virginia's coastal plains such as ibis, herons, and egrets. The gift shop is full of neat stuff along the lines of ant farms and glowing, floating plastic jellyfish. Also glowing are Virginia's starry night skies, projected in the Abbitt Planetarium onto a 30-foot dome above 71 specially designed seats. See the website for stargazing times as well as laser shows.

The museum (524 J. Clyde Morris Blvd., 757/595-1900, www.thevlm.org, 9 A.M.–5 P.M. Mon.–Sat., noon–5 P.M. Sun., extended hours Memorial Day to Labor Day, $15 adults, $12 children 3–12, with admission to planetarium $19 adults, $16 children) also offers various educational programs and outings, including Chesapeake Bay eco-safaris.

Huntington Park

At the east end of the James River Bridge (Rte. 258), Huntington Park (757/886-7912, www.nnparks.com) is a good spot for lazing around—sunbathers can catch some rays on

the lifeguarded beach, open Memorial Day through Labor Day—or running around. Kids can wear themselves out splashing in the river or playing in **Fort Fun,** a 15,000-square-foot wooden playground overlooking the water. There's even a kids' fishing pier.

The grown-up version is the **James River Bridge Fishing Pier** (757/247-0364, 9 A.M.–11:30 P.M. Sun.–Tues., 24 hours a day Wed.–Sat., Apr.–Nov., $8.50 adults, $6 children, including fishing license), which sells bait and supplies and rents poles. At 0.6 mile, this is one of the longest piers on the East Coast.

Also within the park, the **Virginia War Museum** (9285 Warwick Blvd., 757/247-8523, www.warmuseum.org, 9 A.M.–5 P.M. Mon.–Sat., 1–5 P.M. Sun., $6 adults, $4 children 7–18) displays hundreds of artifacts from centuries of combat. From flintlock pistols to M-16s, sabers to WWII Japanese officers' samurai swords, anything and everything having to do with conflict in all its forms is displayed next to actual pieces of the Dachau concentration camp and the Berlin Wall.

Other Sights

Even more animals live across J. Clyde Morris Boulevard at the **Peninsula SPCA Exotic Sanctuary and Petting Zoo** (757/595-1399, www.peninsulaspca.com/gallery.html, 11 A.M.–5:30 P.M. Mon.–Fri., 10 A.M.–4:30 P.M. Sat., noon–3:30 P.M. Sun., $2 adults, $1 children). A surprising collection of exotic animals, including a Siberian tiger, a jaguar, and an African mandrill (a type of baboon), shares a rear lot with a petting barnyard, home to goats, ducks, sheep, peacocks, and a few nervous llamas. You can't take any of these animals home with you, but you might be inspired to adopt a dog or cat inside.

The history of the transport wing of the U.S. Army (motto: "Nothing happens until something moves") is the subject of the **U.S. Army Transportation Museum** (757/878-1115, www.transchool.eustis.army.mil/museum/museum.html, 9 A.M.–4:30 P.M. Tues.–Sun., free), located on the grounds of Fort Eustis off I-64 exit 250A. If it ever carried men or equipment, it's here, from a Conestoga wagon to Desert Storm Humvees. (Visitors must show a valid ID and vehicle registration to get a visitor pass just inside the gate.)

Accommodations

The **Omni Newport News Hotel** (1000 Omni Blvd., 757/873-6664) has rooms for $110–160, an indoor heated pool, a nightclub, and Mitty's Ristorante, one of the better Italian eateries this side of Hampton Roads. In the growing City Center at Oyster Point development is the 256-room **Newport News Marriott at City Center** (740 Town Center Dr., 757/873-9299), with rooms ranging $140–200.

The smaller-scale **Mulberry Inn** (16890 Warwick Blvd., 757/887-3000 or 800/223-0404, www.mulberryinnva.com) has a total of 101 rooms and efficiencies for $90–140. In the same complex, there's a **Holiday Inn Express** (16890 Warwick Blvd., 757/887-3300) offering 57 rooms for $90–130.

The **Boxwood Inn** (10 Elmhurst St., 757/888-8854, www.boxwood-inn.com) began as the early-1900s home of Simon Curtis, railroad baron and unofficial "boss man" of Warwick County. Set along the train tracks that made Curtis his fortune, the building was gradually expanded and altered into a general store, boardinghouse, post office, and county hall of records, until its latest turn as a bed-and-breakfast with four rooms for $105–145. In addition to breakfast, innkeepers Kathy and Derek Hulick serve Friday dinners by reservation only. If you're lucky, you might catch one of their themed dinners for larger groups, which run the gamut from a 1950s sock hop to an antebellum plantation dinner.

Food

Swing by the historic Hilton Village neighborhood to find **99 Main** (99 Main St., 757/599-9885, dinner Tues.–Sat.), voted one of the top fine-dining eateries in Hampton Roads. Whether you sit in the formal dining room or the smaller bar room, entrées like grilled tuna and sea scallops and truffles ($15–30) are always terrific.

On the James River Fishing Pier sits the **Crab Shack** (7601 River Rd., 757/245-2722, lunch and dinner daily), with a window-lined dining room and outdoor deck overlooking the James River. Fresh soft-shell crabs and the catch of the day come in sandwiches ($7–10) and on platters ($17–20). If you think it can't get any fresher, try the sushi and sashimi ($2–4) at **Kappo Nara** (550 Oyster Point Rd., 757/249-5396, dinner daily).

Al Fresco (11710 Jefferson Ave., 757/873-0644, lunch Mon.–Fri., dinner Mon.–Sat.) comes recommended for authentic Italian fare (especially the lobster ravioli), with dinner entrées in the $12–22 range.

Information

The **Newport News Visitor Center** (13560 Jefferson Ave., 757/886-7777 or 888/493-7386, www.newport-news.org, 9 A.M.–5 P.M. daily) is at the entrance to Newport News Park at I-64 exit 250B.

Getting There

Newport News is connected to Hampton, Norfolk, Virginia Beach, Portsmouth, and Chesapeake by **Hampton Roads Transit** (757/222-6100, www.gohrt.com). Call or check the website for routes, hours, and fares. **Amtrak** (9304 Warwick Blvd., 757/245-3589) is in Huntington Park, the closest station to Hampton Roads, and has shuttle bus service to Norfolk and Virginia Beach. To reach the terminal of the **Newport News-Williamsburg International Airport** (757/877-0221, www.nnwairport.com), turn onto Bland Boulevard off Jefferson Avenue (Rte. 143) near I-64 exit 255.

HAMPTON

The oldest English-speaking community in America leapt into the modern age with the seven *Mercury* astronauts, who trained at Langley Air Force Base on gear supplied by NASA's Langley Research Center. Hampton (pop. 145,000) overflows with history, especially African American history. The city boasts an attractive modern waterfront jammed with masts and fishing boats.

History

A settlement of Kecoughtan (KICK-o-tan) Indians was overrun on July 9, 1610, by a band of settlers sent by Capt. John Smith to build a fort at the mouth of the James River. (The city recognizes the date of this skirmish as its official Founders Day, and in 2010 celebrated its 400th anniversary.) While Jamestown was founded first, Hampton's population stayed put, thus it wins the title of the nation's oldest continuously settled English community.

Fort Henry and Fort Charles both came in handy when relations with the native tribe went downhill. Formally established and named in 1680, Hampton was plagued by pirates during its early years. In 1718, Lt. Robert Maynard is said to have captured and killed Edward Teach, aka Blackbeard, and displayed his head at the entrance to the bay as a warning to other pirates.

Hampton was spared during the Revolutionary War but attacked and occupied by the British in 1813. The Civil War ironclads *Monitor* and *Virginia* battled within sight of Fort Story in March 1862, eight months after Hampton's inhabitants had burned most of the city to the ground to prevent its falling into Federal hands.

A rich vein of African American history in the area began in August 1619 with the arrival of British America's first shipment of "20 and odd" Africans to Old Point Comfort and continued with the founding of the Hampton Normal and Agricultural Institute (now Hampton University) in 1868.

Hampton Carousel

This ornate merry-go-round ($2 pp) graced an amusement park on Buckroe Beach 1921–1985. Now located on Hampton's downtown waterfront, it's been fully restored and enclosed from the elements, with all the original paintings, mirrors, and organ music intact. From Memorial Day to Labor Day, the carousel is open 11 A.M.–5 P.M. daily, until 7 P.M. Thursday–Sunday. During the off-season, it's open weekends noon–5 P.M. Call the Virginia Air and Space Center (757/727-0900) for more details.

Virginia Air and Space Center

Imagine an airplane hangar opening like a beetle's wings and you'll have a good picture of Hampton Roads' temple of aeronautics, full to its curving roof with jets, spacecraft, and all the high-tech gizmos that keep them in the air. The *Apollo 12* command module and a three-billion-year-old moon rock commemorate the Space Race, and dozens of hands-on displays explain the principles of flight and space travel. You can have your height scanned electronically, try to keep lunch down in the tri-axis astronaut trainer, or catch a movie in the five-story IMAX theater. The **Hampton Roads History Center** upstairs traces the area's past and includes what archaeologists believe is a pirate's skeleton.

The Air and Space Center (600 Settlers Landing Rd., 757/727-0900, www.vasc.org, 10 A.M.–5 P.M. daily, to 7 P.M. Thurs.–Sun., Memorial Day to Labor Day, shorter hours off-season, $9.50 adults, $7.50 children) offers combination admission with an IMAX movie ($15 adults, $12 children).

Air Power Park

If you're still hungry for more planes, this outdoor park (413 W. Mercury Blvd., 757/727-8311, 9 A.M.–4:30 P.M. daily, free) should do the trick: It's one of the largest privately owned collections of aircraft in the country. Plenty of airborne lethality is on display, from a Nike surface-to-air missile to supersonic jets.

Hampton History Museum

Hampton's story of place is told through 7,000 square feet of exhibits, including two interactive galleries, the Kecoughtan Indian Gallery and the Port Hampton Gallery, unveiled since the doors opened in 2003. The museum (120 Old Hampton Ln., 757/727-1610, www.hampton.gov/history_museum, 10 A.M.–5 P.M. Mon.–Sat., 1–5 P.M. Sun., $5 adults, $4 children 4–12) focuses on the Civil War and the periods before and after, including the Battle of Big Bethel and the burning of Hampton.

St. John's Church

Elizabeth City Parish, the oldest continuous

English-speaking parish in the country, was established in the same year Europeans arrived at Hampton. This small cruciform church (100 W. Queens Way, 757/722-2567, 9 A.M.–3 P.M. Mon.–Fri., 9 A.M.–noon Sat., free) is the congregation's fourth, erected in 1728. Eight-foot-thick walls are graced by stained-glass windows dating to 1883, one of which portrays the baptism of Pocahontas. Take a minute to wander the surrounding graveyard, with its ornate monuments and Confederate tombstones.

Hampton University

The story of America's foremost black university (757/727-5000, www.hamptonu.edu) goes back to the Civil War, when escaped slaves sought refuge at Union-held Fort Monroe. Federal officers declared the runaways "contraband of war" to ensure their safety, and in 1868 Gen. Samuel Chapman Armstrong answered their pleas for education by opening the Hampton Normal and Agricultural Institute in the center of the city. Initially consisting of only three teachers and 15 students, Hampton University has grown to 5,700 students, counting Booker T. Washington among its many distinguished alumni. Still standing near the entrance is Emancipation Oak, under whose branches slaves once labored over the alphabet and the Emancipation Proclamation was first read to the local populace.

The galleries of the **Hampton University Museum** (757/727-5308, http://museum.hamptonu.edu, 8 A.M.–5 P.M. Mon.–Fri., noon–4 P.M. Sat., free) hold 9,000 pieces of African American, Native American, Asian, and Pacific art, including works by John T. Biggers, Elizabeth Catlett, and Henry O. Tanner's *The Banjo Lesson*. The museum store sells handcrafted ethnic art. In 1997 the collection was moved to the Huntington Building on Frissell Avenue, a former beaux arts library renovated to the tune of $5 million.

Fort Monroe

Fort Monroe is the largest stone fortification ever built in the United States, constructed in 1819–1834 at Old Point Comfort to protect the strategic entrance to Chesapeake Bay. Edgar Allan Poe was stationed here 1828–1829, and Robert E. Lee was here 1831–1834 as a second lieutenant and engineer. Manned by 6,000 soldiers, Monroe was the only fort in the upper South that remained in Union hands during the Civil War. In May 1862, Abraham Lincoln visited "Fort Freedom," two months after Federal troops watched the *Monitor* and the *Virginia* shell it out from the ramparts.

Today—well, at least until 2011—the fort is headquarters for the U.S. Army Training and Doctrine Command. It's still surrounded by a moat with a bridge wide enough for only a single car. But change is coming to Fort Monroe. Due to Department of Defense recommendations for moving or closing bases, which Congress approved in 2005, the army will vacate the property by September 2011. What next? Many locals wonder the same thing. At the time of writing the National Park Service had committed to overseeing a portion of the historic fort, and museums from Richmond to Martinsville were eyeing the property.

In the meantime, visitors can still walk around the walls for the view of Norfolk across the water and visit the **Casemate Museum** (757/727-3391, 10:30 A.M.–4:30 P.M. daily, free), in whose cool, dank chambers Jefferson Davis was imprisoned for six months after the end of the war. Displays on the history of the fort and coastal artillery include relics of Davis's stay, including his intricate meerschaum pipe. Unquestionably the oldest witness to history on base, and all its comings and goings, is the Algernourne Oak, a nearly 500-year-old tree growing on the parade field.

Entertainment and Recreation

Buckroe Beach (757/850-5134) is a wide, clean stretch of sand on the Chesapeake Bay. Outdoor movies are held at the waterfront pavilion on Tuesdays in the summer; beach-music favorites are on the bill every Sunday. You can rent watercraft in the summer.

Racing vehicles of every stripe roar through **Langley Speedway** (3165 N. Armistead Ave.,

757/865-7223, www.langley-speedway.com) during its yearly schedule of races.

Head down to the public piers near the visitors center to find the **Miss Hampton II** (757/722-9102 or 888/757-2628, www.miss hamptoncruises.com), a double-decker motor boat that explores the Chesapeake Bay on sightseeing cruises Tuesday–Sunday April–October ($22.50 adults, $11.50 children). On sunny days, it passes the Norfolk Naval Base and stops at Fort Wool, a pre–Civil War citadel built on a 15-acre man-made island.

For an evening out, it's hard to beat the **Hampton Coliseum** (757/838-4230, www .hamptoncoliseum.org), which has welcomed everyone from the Rolling Stones to Metallica over the years. (The Coliseum's "Elvis Door" was cut into the side of the arena in the 1970s so the King could escape straight to his limo after the show.) **Marker 20** (21 E. Queens Way, 757/726-9410) often hosts live music.

Events

Hampton's big yearly event is the **Hampton Jazz Festival** (www.hamptonjazzfestival .com) at the Coliseum in late June, boasting some of the world's best musicians. It's shifting toward more soul, blues, and pop; performers in previous years included Aretha Franklin, Ray Charles, and B. B. King. Hotel rooms fill up months ahead of the three-day festival, so plan accordingly.

Street Fest brings local music, eats, and kids' events to Queens Way near the visitors center on Saturday evenings throughout the summer. The **Hampton Cup Regatta** (www .hamptoncupregatta.org) in mid-August is the oldest ongoing race of its kind in the country. Numerous classes of hydroplane boats hit up to 170 mph on their way from the Mercury Boulevard Bridge to Fort Monroe. In early September, the Chesapeake Bay is cause for celebration during **Hampton Bay Days** (www .baydays.com), the city's biggest event. Held the weekend after Labor Day, it includes carnivals, seafood, sports, music, crab races, water events, and fireworks.

Accommodations

The **Arrow Inn** (3361 Commander Shepard Blvd.—which used to be 7 Semple Farm Rd., 757/865-0300 or 800/833-2520, www.arrow inn.com) is a motel near the Langley Speedway with rooms for $40–60. Only a few blocks away from the Hampton Coliseum, the **La Quinta Inn** (2138 W. Mercury Blvd., 757/827-8680) has rooms for $85–135. Nearby you'll find a **Comfort Inn** (1916 Coliseum Dr., 757/827-5052) with rooms for $70–160. The **Crowne Plaza Hampton Marina** (700 Settlers Landing Rd., 757/727-9700, www.hamptonmarinahotel.com) offers waterfront accommodations for $120–160, with suites for twice that. The Crowne Plaza's dining options include an upscale grill, a sports bar, and a casual waterside bistro.

RVs can camp at **Gosnold's Hope Park** (757/850-5116) for $11 per night with water and electric hookups. It's north of downtown Hampton off Little Back River Road, and open year-round, but can get a bit rowdy on game days at the nearby sports fields or the Hampton Supertrack, a BMX racecourse.

Food

Look for the Dionysian painting on the outer wall of **La Bodega** (22 Wine St., 757/722-8466, breakfast and lunch Mon.–Sat., $5–8). Homemade bread and signature sandwiches around $7 are among the edible offerings at this gourmet deli and espresso bar. **Anna's Italian Pizza** (1979 E. Pembroke Ave., 757/723-3593, lunch and dinner Tues.–Sun.) serves dependable Italian fare—subs, pastas, seafood, salads, and the obvious pizza. Prices range $7–18.

For fresh seafood, you could do much worse than **Marker 20** (21 E. Queens Way, 757/726-9410, lunch and dinner daily). All the fruits of the Chesapeake Bay range $10–19, and there are special late-night and Sunday brunch menus as well. (Make your own mimosas and Bloody Marys for brunch.) Live music, microbrews, and covered outdoor dining make this a favorite local place to take guests. **The Grey Goose** (101 W. Queens Way, 757/723-7978, breakfast Mon.–Fri., lunch Mon.–Sat.) is a continental-style restaurant with homemade soups, salads, sandwiches, biscuits, and desserts ($6–9).

Information

Hampton's **visitors center** (120 Old Hampton Ln., 757/727-1102, 9 A.M.–5 P.M. daily) is located under the same roof as the Hampton History Museum. The Hampton Convention & Visitors Bureau is another good resource (757/722-1222, www.visithampton.com).

Getting There

Hampton is connected to Norfolk, Newport News, Virginia Beach, Portsmouth, and Chesapeake by **Hampton Roads Transit** (757/222-6100, www.gohrt.com). Call or check HRT's website for routes, hours, and fares. There's a **Greyhound/Trailways** terminal (757/722-9861) located at 2 West Pembroke Avenue and Jefferson Avenue (Rte. 143).

Norfolk and Vicinity

Norfolk (pop. 234,000), Virginia's second-largest city and the unofficial hub of Hampton Roads, is more than home to the world's largest naval base. The city also gives the region a "real" downtown and city-style skyline, and it is home to a galaxy of great restaurants, outstanding museums, five colleges and universities, and enough nightlife and shopping to keep even visiting sailors happy—now that most of the off-color waterfront joints have closed.

Norfolk is a surprisingly pleasant city, with a walkable waterfront marketplace, a $36 million cruise terminal, and plenty of green parks and blue water in every direction. (By the way, it's pronounced NOR-fik—or NAW-fik if you want to sound like a true old-time local.)

History

The original town site of about 500 acres was bought near the turn of the 18th century for 10,000 pounds of tobacco. It quickly became one of Colonial Virginia's largest trade centers, sending out tobacco, flour, meat, and lumber to be exchanged for sugar and molasses in the West Indies. With a spring at Main and Church Streets the only source of drinking water, visiting sailors naturally steered for the taverns (and have been doing so, more or less, ever since).

With a little more than 1,000 residents by the latter part of the 18th century, Norfolk almost ceased to exist on New Year's Day 1776,

when an 11-hour British bombardment leveled two-thirds of the city. Within two months, colonists had destroyed the rest to prevent it from sheltering Lord Dunmore's soldiers. Only a few brick structures were left standing in "chimney town," including the cannon-scarred walls of St. Paul's Church.

Such a great location couldn't go to waste, though, and Norfolk soon rebuilt itself into the largest town in Virginia. Many of its 7,000 inhabitants worked on the docks and in the warehouses that exchanged produce from the Piedmont for goods from abroad. Some historians blame the economic jealousy of upriver cities for Norfolk's failure to become a great ocean port akin to Boston or New York.

Tens of thousands of Confederate troops stationed nearby couldn't keep Norfolk, along with Portsmouth and Suffolk, from falling into the hands of the Federals in March 1862. The first steps to becoming the world's largest coal port came with the first load, which arrived in 1882 on the Norfolk & Western Railroad. In 1907, the Jamestown Exhibition drew national attention to Norfolk and planted the seeds of the naval base in a few abandoned buildings used for offices and barracks. Three years later, Eugene Ely made the first airplane flight from a ship (an honor turned down by the Wright brothers).

A friendly force of soldiers, sailors, and officers invaded Norfolk during World War I, prompting

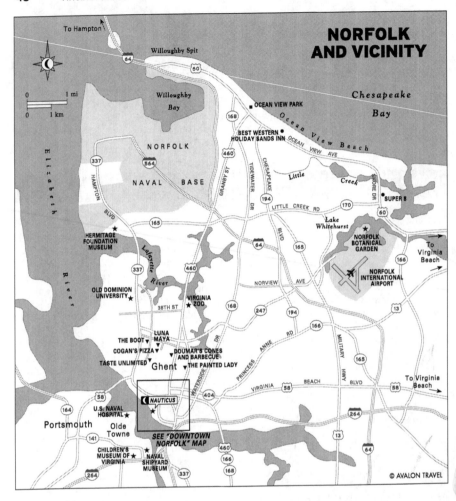

construction of a working base in 1917. Huge ships steamed in and out of Hampton Roads, dropping off men for training and R&R and picking up munitions turned out by the thousands. By the end of the war, Norfolk counted 34,000 enlisted residents and was well on its way to becoming synonymous with the U.S. Navy. East Main Street was famous worldwide for its bars, burlesque halls, and tattoo parlors. (The last were banned from 1950 to 2006.)

Even with the base closings of the 1990s, Norfolk is still the world's largest naval center. A recent downtown renaissance cleaned up seedy sections of the waterfront and saw the creation of a 12,000-seat baseball stadium for the AAA Norfolk Tides and the futuristic NAUTICUS maritime center. A 260-foot whale mural gracing a parking garage on Waterside Drive illustrates the revival. The Ghent neighborhood, once one of Norfolk's classiest zip codes, has been rescued from a mid-century decline and turned into a hot spot of boutiques, fine restaurants, and historic homes within walking distance of Old Dominion University.

SIGHTS
◖ NAUTICUS

The $52 million maritime-themed science center was opened in 1994 to much fanfare (and some controversy over the price tag). Designed to resemble an aircraft carrier—down to a Blue Angel fighter landing on top—this high-tech

gallery offers children and adults a plethora of interactive displays on all things nautical, from ship design to cleaning up after an oil spill.

Experience warfare at sea in the AEGIS theater, which simulates the bridge of a destroyer. Beautiful tropical fish and moray eels flit through aquariums near a touch tank and working aquatic laboratories. On the 2nd floor, the **Hampton Roads Naval Museum** covers two centuries of local naval history through archaeology, models, and photographs.

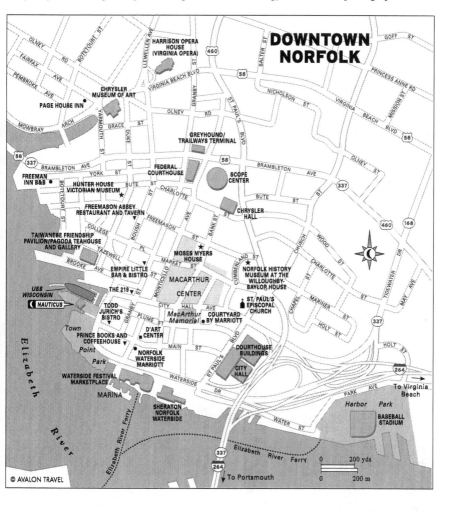

The latest addition to the Naval Museum is parked next door and easily as big as the center itself. The 887-foot **USS *Wisconsin*** is one of four Iowa-class battleships in the U.S. Navy, and it's almost unbelievably big. Nine 16-inch guns saw action in World War II, Korea, and the Persian Gulf. Some 2,700 men served onboard during World War II—1,000 more than there were room for, leading to such crowding that one sailor searched for a friend for three days, then ended up sending him a postcard in frustration. Because the navy has to have two battleships on call at all times (currently this one and the USS *Iowa*), the *Wisconsin* could technically be called into service at any time, thus the lower decks remain sealed off to visitors.

NAUTICUS (1 Waterside Dr., 757/664-1000 or 800/664-1080, www.nauticus.org, 10 A.M.–5 P.M. daily, $19 adults, $15 children 4–12) has a gift shop and a cafeteria on its 1st floor, open to anyone who crosses the "gangplank" entrance ramp.

MacArthur Memorial

Norfolk's 19th-century City Hall, a neoclassic monolith designed by the same architect as the U.S. Capitol, was chosen as the final resting place for General Douglas MacArthur (1880–1964), one of the past century's most intriguing military figures, who is buried in the building's rotunda (757/441-2965, www.macarthurmemorial.org, 10 A.M.–5 P.M. Mon.–Sat., 11 A.M.–5 P.M. Sun., free).

St. Paul's Episcopal Church

The only building to survive the leveling of Norfolk in 1776 stands in an island of trees and ancient gravestones amid the clutter and clamor of downtown. The first church on this site was built in 1639; this one dates to 1739 and still has a British cannonball embedded in its south wall. The church (St. Paul's Blvd. and City Hall Ave., 757/627-4353, www.saintpaulsnorfolk.com, 9 A.M.–4 P.M. Mon.–Sat., Sun. services, free) still supports an active Episcopal parish.

Chrysler Museum of Art

Named one of the 20 best art museums in the country by the *Wall Street Journal,* the Chrysler houses the personal collection of Walter Chrysler, who ran one of the "big three" car companies and built New York's Chrysler Building. The collection ranges from pre-Columbian to modern, touching on Greco-

You have to see the USS *Wisconsin*, parked next to the NAUTICUS maritime center, to grasp its size.

The Torch Bearers, by sculptor Anna Hyatt Huntington, dramatically marks the entrance to the Chrysler Museum of Art.

Roman, Asian, Islamic, Egyptian, and Indian along the way. Works by Mary Cassatt, Paul Gauguin, and Edward Hopper hang alongside an outstanding collection of decorative glass, including dozens of gorgeous Tiffany lamps, windows, and the famous flower-form vase.

The museum (245 W. Olney Rd., 757/664-6200, www.chrysler.org, 10 A.M.–5 P.M. Thurs.–Sat., 10 A.M.–9 P.M. Wed., noon–5 P.M. Sun., permanent exhibit is free) also administers the Moses Myers and Willoughby-Baylor historic houses. **Cuisine and Company** (757/333-6291, lunch Wed.–Sun., dinner Wed.) serves light lunch fare, coffee, and dessert—and on Wednesday, dinner specials.

Historic Houses

The **Moses Myers House** (Freemason and Bank Sts., 757/441-1526, 10 A.M.–4 P.M. Wed.–Sat., noon–4 P.M. Sun., free) was built 1789–1791 by one of Norfolk's first Jewish residents, a consul and merchant originally from New York. His family lived here until 1931, when the house was opened as a museum concentrating on the lifestyle and traditions of Virginia's early Jewish immigrants. Most of the furniture, including a beautiful tall case clock, is original.

The furnishings and medical paraphernalia collected by the family of James Wilson Hunter fill the **Hunter House Victorian Museum** (240 W. Freemason St., 757/623-9814, www.hunterhousemuseum.org, 10 A.M.–3:30 P.M. Wed.–Sat., 12:30–3:30 P.M. Sun., Apr.–Dec., $5 adults, $1 children). Guided tours leave every half hour. Don't miss the stained-glass windows and the turn-of-the-20th-century EKG machine.

A blend of Georgian and Federal styles characterizes the structure that now holds the **Norfolk History Museum at the Willoughby-Baylor House** (601 E. Freemason St., 757/441-1526, 10 A.M.–4 P.M. Wed.–Sat., noon–4 P.M. Sun., free), restored to reflect the middle-class 18th-century life of Capt. William Willoughby's family. Cooking and medicinal herbs have been replanted in the kitchen garden. Tours are given on the hour until 3 or 4 P.M. depending on the season.

Hermitage Foundation Museum

The 12-acre summer retreat of William and Florence Sloane, built 1908–1932 on the shore of the Lafayette River, now houses one of the largest private collections of Asian art in the country. The mock Tudor house is a wonder, filled with hidden doors and stairways and incredible wood carvings by Charles Woodsend. Then there's the collection: 1,400-year-old Chinese marble Buddhas, unique Persian prayer rugs, and minutely detailed Chinese and Japanese snuffboxes. Other ancient cultures are represented by glass vials to catch the tears of Roman mourners, intricately carved Spanish *varqueños* (traveling desks), Bronze Age burial containers for food, and more.

The museum (7637 North Shore Rd., 757/423-2052, www.hermitagefoundation.org, 10 A.M.–5 P.M. Mon.–Tues. and Fri.–Sat., 1–5 P.M. Sun., $5 adults, $2 children 6–18) offers mandatory tours that last one hour. The lush, wooded grounds are free.

Norfolk Naval Base

The home of NATO's Atlantic operations and the U.S. Atlantic Fleet—all 150 ships and 100,000 workers—the Norfolk Naval Base stretches for 15 miles along the Elizabeth River and Willoughby Bay. Visitors can ogle monstrous aircraft carriers, amphibious assault vessels, submarines, cruisers, and destroyers on narrated bus tours ($10 adults, $5 children), which leave on a seasonally varying schedule from the Waterside; call the Naval Base Tour Office (757/444-7955) for details. Two-hour harbor boat tours leave from NAUTICUS aboard the *Victory Rover* (1 Waterside Dr., 757/627-7406, www.navalbasecruises.com) for $18 adults and $10 children.

Virginia Zoo

A century old, this is the state's largest zoo, with 350 animals in its collection. Most popular is a special 10-acre African exhibit, with African elephants, white rhinos, lions, zebras, giraffes, meerkats, and warthogs displayed in natural surroundings near a replica of an African village. The zoo (3500 Granby St., 757/441-2374, www.virginiazoo.org, 10 A.M.–5 P.M. daily, $7 adults, $5 children) offers special children's events, including summer safaris, crafts, and games. Changing exhibits pass through regularly.

Norfolk Botanical Garden

This is the perfect antidote to Hampton Roads' urban sprawl—155 acres of trees, shrubs, and flowering plants covering the area between the Norfolk International Airport and Lake Whitehurst. It's easy to spend a whole day wandering among beds brimming with so many varieties of plants that something's almost always in bloom. Every known variety of azalea—250 in all—blooms March–May, followed by the 4,000 plants in the Bicentennial Rose Garden. Add 500 camellias and one of the largest collections of rhododendrons east of the Mississippi, and you have a flower lover's nirvana. More than 30 special gardens include a tropical plant pavilion, Colonial herb garden, and a unique garden in a bog, where unfortunate Confederate POWs were held during the Civil War.

The gardens (6700 Azalea Garden Rd., 757/441-5830, www.norfolkbotanicalgarden.org, 9 A.M.–7 P.M. daily, to 5 P.M. Oct.–Apr., $7 adults, $5 children 3–18) offer 12 miles of trails winding through the greenery, including the Fragrance Garden Trail for visitors with impaired vision. You can walk or drive the paths (no bikes) or take a tram tour for free. A boat tour on the lake costs $4 adults, $2 children. In the main building, you'll find a horticultural gift shop and the **Garden House Café,** with a patio over the Japanese garden. Kids love the "children's adventure garden," called the World of Wonders, with fountains, herbs from around the world, and the "dirt factory."

It's no surprise that the gardens are popular with wedding parties and, especially in late April, with picnickers, who flock for the azalea-themed **Norfolk NATO Festival.** The four-day event celebrates Norfolk's role in NATO, honoring a different country every year and ending with the coronation of an Azalea Queen in a special garden pavilion. (The only thing to disturb the peace of the place are the airplanes taking off overhead from the airport next door, but at least there's an overlook to get a good view.)

ENTERTAINMENT AND RECREATION

To find out what's going on around Norfolk, pick up a free copy of the *Port Folio* entertainment weekly or the Friday *Preview* section of the *Virginian Pilot.*

Nightlife

The **Tap House Grill** (931 W. 21st St., 757/627-9172) has a young crowd and a long list of microbrews to go with live music most evenings. **The Banque** (1849 E. Little Creek Rd., 757/480-3600) has been voted Club of the Year by the Virginia Country Music Association several times for its huge dance floor and quality bookings. The **NorVa** (317 Monticello Ave., 757/627-4547, www.thenorva.com) is a mid-sized concert venue with room for 1,500 people and a great sound system.

The beautiful people are reported to congregate at **Havana** (255 Granby St., 757/627-5800). In Ghent, the **Naro Expanded Cinema** (1507 Colley Ave., 757/625-6276, www.narocinema .com, $8) shows independent flicks and the cult classic *Rocky Horror Picture Show.*

Performing Arts

Norfolk's eye-catching **Scope** arena (201 E. Brambleton Ave., 757/664-6464, www.seven venues.com) can seat more than 12,000 for concerts, ice shows, and circuses. The more intimate **Chrysler Hall** (215 St. Paul's Blvd., 757/664-6464) is reminiscent of D.C.'s Kennedy Center and hosts the **Virginia Symphony** (757/892-6366, www.virginia symphony.org) as well as Broadway shows and an annual pops series. The symphony has been performing since the 1920s and gives more than 140 concerts per year.

The **Virginia Opera** (866/673-7282, www .vaopera.org) is the official company of the Commonwealth, performing at the 1,600-seat Harrison Opera House (160 E. Virginia Beach Blvd.), as well as in Richmond and Fairfax. Six productions per year are on the schedule for the **Virginia Stage Company** (757/627-1234, www.vastage.com) September–April at the cozy Wells Theater on Monticello Avenue. Contact **Ballet Virginia** (757/446-1401, www .balletvirginia.org) for its current schedule.

Spectator Sports

The AAA **Norfolk Tides** (757/622-2222, www .norfolktides.com) aren't the only ones enjoying the Harbor Park stadium. The **Hits at the Park** restaurant helped earn the park a reputation as one of the best minor-league ballparks in the country—perfect for this farm team for the Baltimore Orioles, and before that the New York Mets. (The Tides have already produced stars such as Dwight Gooden and Darryl Strawberry.) Partners with the Washington Capitols, the **Norfolk Admirals** hockey team (757/640-1212, www.norfolkadmirals.com) competes in the East Coast Hockey League in the Scope arena October–March.

On the Water

Vacation homes and inexpensive apartment-hotels line the seven miles of **Ocean View Beach** on the Chesapeake Bay, with public bathrooms, picnic facilities, and a 1,600-foot pier where you can rent fishing and crabbing gear. It's a quieter alternative to Virginia Beach's crowds, and lifeguards keep an eye out during the summer, even though there's no undertow. Ocean View Beach Park hosts free movies, concerts, and food festivals May–August; contact Norfolk Festevents (757/441-2345, www.fest eventsva.org) for a schedule.

Certified instructor Randy Gore runs **Kayak Nature Tours** (757/480-1999 or 888/669-8368, www.kayaknaturetours.net), which offers beginning and intermediate kayak classes, as well as rolling clinics. The focus is on 2.5-hour local trips ($50–55 pp), but he also does longer trips to the Back Bay, the Eastern Shore, and the Great Dismal Swamp ($75–115).

Cruises and Tours

Sightseeing, dining, and fun-time cruises

aboard the sleek *Spirit of Norfolk* (866/304-2469, www.spiritofnorfolk.com) leave from the Waterside year-round. Choices range from moonlight cruises to lunch and dinner trips ($60–80). Call for information on tours of the Naval Base.

Standing 135 feet tall, the red-sailed *American Rover* (757/627-7245, www.american rover.com) is the largest topsail passenger schooner flying the stars and stripes. Daily tours of Hampton Roads nautical landmarks past and present run April–October from the Waterside dock for $16 adults, $10 children under 12. There are also sunset ($25/$15) cruises and party cruises ($12) after dark with a full bar and music.

Hampton Roads Transit (757/222-6100, www.gohrt.com) operates a Paddlewheel Ferry that runs between the Norfolk and Portsmouth waterfronts. It's a quick way to port-hop and a cheap way to see the waterfront ($1.50 one-way).

SHOPPING

Designed by the same architectural team responsible for Baltimore's Harborplace and Richmond's Sixth Street Marketplace, Norfolk's **Waterside Festival Marketplace** (333 Waterside Dr., www.watersidemarket place.com) has dozens of shops selling African art, Southwestern jewelry, clothes, herbs, and Virginiana. Art exhibits and music performances pass through various public spaces, and there are plenty of places to stop for a bite. The complex also has bars, restaurants, and a visitors center. In a similar vein, smack in the center of downtown is the gargantuan **MacArthur Center,** a shopping mall with 140 well-known chain stores and eateries and an 18-screen multiplex.

Prince Books and Coffeehouse (109 E. Main St., 757/622-9223) has an excellent selection and friendly service, along with a coffee shop for sipping while perusing your latest find. Also downtown is the **d'Art Center** (208 E. Main St., 757/625-4211, www.d-art center.org, 10 A.M.–5 P.M. Tues.–Sat., 1–5 P.M. Sun.) in the Selden Arcade, home to 40 artists laboring over everything from ceramics to calligraphy. You can stop by to chat or browse; call the center for information on art classes and changing exhibits.

Norfolk's trendiest shopping neighborhood is historic Ghent, centered on Colley Avenue and 21st Street. Here you'll find antiques stores such as **Merlo's** (810 Granby St., 757/622-2699) and upscale consignment stores like **2nd Act Consignment** (110-A W. 21st St., 757/622-1533).

EVENTS

With as many annual celebrations as any city in the state, Norfolk takes its festivals seriously. It even has an office devoted just to scheduling and information, called **Festevents** (120 W. Main St., 757/441-2345, www.festevents va.org). Unless indicated otherwise, all events are held among the trees in the pleasant Town Point Park on the Waterfront. Along with those listed here, the park hosts free **Big Bands on the Bay** concerts and dancing May–August. Sailing fans will want to keep an eye out for regular **tall-ship visitations,** when ships from as far away as South America dock at the park. When you climb aboard you'll find the crews are happy to show you around.

March brings the **ShamRock 'N Roll** party over St. Patrick's Day. In early May, the **Norfolk NATO Festival,** formerly the International Azalea Festival, ends with an air show featuring the Blue Angels, barnstormers, and freefall teams celebrating Norfolk's importance to NATO. The festival culminates in the coronation of an Azalea Queen. From late April to late May, the **Virginia Arts Festival** (www .virginiaartsfest.com) attracts world-class performers such as Itzhak Perlman and the Russian National Ballet for a series of concerts in Norfolk, Hampton, Portsmouth, and Virginia Beach.

Early June's **Harborfest** is Norfolk's biggest celebration, attracting 100,000 people for water and air shows, live entertainment, fireworks, and seafood the first weekend of the month. A highlight is the Parade of Sails, a procession of fully rigged sailboats through the harbor.

Zydeco and crawdads arrive in late June

during the **Bayou Boogaloo,** followed by the **Norfolk Jazz Festival** in late July. Giant puppets, costumed characters, and theater shows mark the **Virginia Children's Festival** in early October.

In mid-October 25 Virginia wineries are featured during the **Town Point Virginia Wine Festival,** which sets the stage for the Halloween **Masquerade in Ghent.**

ACCOMMODATIONS
$50-100
Only a short walk from the Chesapeake Bay and Ocean View Beach is a **Super 8** (7940 Shore Dr., 757/588-7888, $90–100). The beachfront **Best Western Holiday Sands Inn** (1330 E. Ocean View Ave., 757/583-2621, $80–140) also has an outdoor pool and fitness center.

$100-150
The **America's Best Value Inn** (235 N. Military Hwy., 757/461-6600, $90–150) near I-264 has a pool, sauna, and gym. There's also the **Crowne Plaza Norfolk** (700 Monticello Ave., 757/627-5555) with 204 rooms starting at $140.

$150-200
Carl Albero runs the restored 1899 Georgian Revival mansion near the Chrysler Museum now known as the 【 **Page House Inn** (323 Fairfax Ave., 757/625-5033 or 800/599-7659, www.pagehouseinn.com). It's furnished with four-poster beds, claw-foot tubs, and 19th-century artwork. Four rooms ($150–170) and three suites ($175–230), including the Bathe Suite with its gas-log fireplace and sunken hot tub, are available in the house. Guests can enjoy the basement billiard room and yard games on the lawn.

The **Courtyard by Marriott** (520 Plume St., 757/963-6000, $140–170) is centrally located downtown, offering a heated indoor pool and valet parking.

$200-250
The elegant rooms at the 【 **Freemason Inn Bed and Breakfast** (411 W. York St., 757/963-7000 or 866/388-1897, www.freemasoninn.com, $145–245) have names like Sir York and East India Tea Co. and come with accoutrements like plush bathrobes and clawfoot tubs. This narrow place was opened by the lawyer whose office is next door, and the 19th-century building has been beautifully restored. It's known for its three-course gourmet candlelight breakfasts. (When's the last time you had dessert before noon?)

Some of the rooms at the 24-story **Norfolk Waterside Marriott** (235 E. Main St., 757/627-4200, $150–220) have views of the Elizabeth River just outside. It offers all the amenities business travelers expect—concierge service, exercise rooms, valet service—and its steak house serves lunch and dinner.

Over $250
Also downtown near the water is the **Sheraton Norfolk Waterside** (777 Waterside Dr., 757/622-6664, $170–200), with 468 rooms and nine suites. It's near the Waterside Marketplace, with great views and an outdoor pool.

FOOD
From cones made on the world's first ice cream–cone machine to dinner in a restored abbey, the city has it covered—and with the headquarters of People for the Ethical Treatment of Animals (PETA) in town, you can be sure there are plenty of vegetarian options.

Snacks and Cafés
Next to NAUTICUS and the USS *Wisconsin* in the ornate Taiwanese Pavilion is the **Pagoda Teahouse and Gallery** (265 Tazewell St., 757/622-0506, lunch Mon.–Sat., dinner Tues.–Sat.), selling tea, coffee, snacks, soups, salads, and sandwiches for $5–7. Heartier entrées like fried tempura shrimp cost up to $14. There are an Asian art gallery and a shop, and an upstairs balcony overlooks the surrounding fountains and flowers. The coffee shop at **Prince Books and Coffeehouse** (109 E. Main St., 757/622-9223, lunch daily) serves pastries, panini, salads, and desserts.

Afternoon tea with scones at **The Painted Lady** (112 E. 17th St., 757/622-5239, lunch and dinner Tues.–Sat., brunch Sun.), a pair of restored Victorian homes painted pink and purple and full of odds and ends, is always fun. Tea is served 2–4 P.M., and there's Teddy Bear Tea for kids.

For healthy gourmet sandwiches for $5–9, look no further than **Taste Unlimited** (1619 Colley Ave., 757/623-7770, lunch daily). This is one of several locations in the Hampton Roads area. It also stocks snacks, chocolates, and wines and will make you a box lunch if you order ahead.

Casual

Thanks in part to the opening of the million-square-foot shopper's paradise called the MacArthur Center nearby, Granby Street has undergone a culinary renaissance of sorts. Case in point is the **Empire Little Bar & Bistro** (245 Granby St., 757/626-3100, dinner daily), which offers bite-sized tapas ($5–12) and more than 30 kinds of martinis and cocktails in a snug, elbow-rubbing setting.

Ghent is the current hot spot outside of downtown for fun, creative dining options. **Cogan's Pizza** (1901 Colonial Ave., 757/627-6428, lunch and dinner daily) serves, unsurprisingly, pizza ($15–20)—it's been voted the best in Hampton Roads—and has dozens of beers on tap. It's an art-filled, tattooed-bartender type of place with a young clientele and an outdoor patio (dogs welcome). It also serves subs and pastas. Along similar lines is **The Boot** (123 W. 21st St., 757/627-2668, dinner Tues.–Sat.). Italian dishes using fresh local ingredients go well with local art on the walls and live music in the evenings. Main dishes are $15–25, with plenty of vegetarian options.

Another good choice in Ghent is **Luna Maya** (2000 Colonial Ave., 757/622-6986, dinner Tues.–Sat.), run by Bolivian sisters in the Corner Shoppes complex. The menu ranges across Latin America, the atmosphere is vibrant, and the prices are reasonable ($11–18 for dinner entrées).

You can munch a bit of history at **❰ Doumar's Cones and Barbecue** (Monticello Ave. and 20th St., 757/627-4163, all meals Mon.–Sat.). "Uncle" Abe Doumar invented the ice cream cone at the 1904 World's Fair, and his original hand-rolling machine is still in use at this true-as-they-come drive-in with famous limeade and curb service (flash your headlights for a server). Even the prices haven't changed in decades: burgers, hot dogs, and barbecue sandwiches are all under $5.

Upscale

A high arched ceiling and stained-glass windows show that the **Freemason Abbey Restaurant & Tavern** (209 W. Freemason St., 757/622-3966, lunch and dinner daily) occupies a real late-19th-century abbey. Daily specials such as lobster, prime rib, and tempura shrimp are $8–18 for lunch and up to $30 for dinner. Lighter choices such as seafood quiche and house sandwiches are also available.

Produce from small, ecologically sound farms goes into the food at **❰ Todd Jurich's Bistro** (150 W. Main St., Ste. 100, 757/622-3210, lunch Mon.–Fri., dinner Mon.–Sat.). Jurich, one of the best chefs in the area, mixes the innovative with the down-home in dishes such as bouillabaisse and Kobe beef short ribs. Entrées range $18–32.

INFORMATION

The **Norfolk Convention & Visitors Bureau** (232 E. Main St., 757/664-6620 or 800/368-3097, www.visitnorfolktoday.com) operates visitors centers in the Waterside complex and at 9401 4th View Street at Ocean View, both open 9 A.M.–5 P.M. daily.

GETTING THERE AND AROUND
Getting There

You can catch a Thruway bus to the Amtrak station at Newport News at Norfolk's **Greyhound/Trailways** terminal (701 Monticello Ave., 757/625-7500). Reach the **Norfolk International Airport** (757/857-3351, www.norfolkairport.com) from I-64 exit 279 to Norview Avenue. **Airport Express** (877/455-7462) will take you there.

Getting Around

Norfolk Electric Transit (NET) (www .norfolk.va.us/visitors/net.asp) runs free buses from Harbor Park to the Harrison Opera House, stopping at Waterside and NAUTICUS along the way. They operate 6:30 A.M.–11 P.M. Monday–Friday, noon–midnight Saturday, and noon–8 P.M. Sunday. Norfolk is connected to Newport News, Hampton, Virginia Beach, Portsmouth, and Chesapeake by **Hampton Roads Transit** (757/222-6100, www.gohrt .com). Call or check its website for routes, hours, and fares. HRT also runs the **Paddle Wheel Ferry** ($1.50) between Waterside in Norfolk and North Landing and High Street in Portsmouth.

PORTSMOUTH

About 100,000 people live in this centuries-old seaport across the Elizabeth River from Norfolk. The nation's oldest naval shipyard bristles with cranes and girders south of the narrow tree-lined brick sidewalks of the Olde Towne district, with more historic buildings than any other city between Alexandria, Virginia, and Charleston, South Carolina.

History

Portsmouth was established in 1752 on the land of a colonist who was executed for participating in Bacon's Rebellion. The Gosport Navy Yard arrived 15 years later, quickly becoming the busiest in the colonies during the Revolutionary War. British soldiers ransacked Portsmouth in 1779 and burned ships in the harbor, but by 1798 the city was again so busy that, according to a witness, "one might walk...to Norfolk on the decks of vessels at anchor." In 1799, the shipyard turned out the *Chesapeake,* the first ship built for the new U.S. government. The British paid another visit during the War of 1812, when 2,600 men landed here only to be beaten back by American troops at forts Norfolk and Nelson (today home to the Navy Medical Center Portsmouth).

Federal forces evacuated the city and burned the naval yard soon after Virginia's entry into the Civil War, allowing Confederate shipbuilders to raise the sunken frigate *Merrimac* and turn her into the CSS *Virginia* in time to battle the Union ironclad *Monitor.* In May 1862, it was the Confederates' turn to torch the city as Union troops moved back in. The country's first battleship, the USS *Texas,* rolled off the docks in 1892, followed by the first American aircraft carrier, the USS *Langley,* in 1922. Portsmouth's docks, well on their way to becoming the largest in the country, were renamed the Norfolk Naval Shipyard in 1945.

Sights

All of Portsmouth's attractions are within easy walking distance of each other. The city's central **Olde Towne** area includes many period homes and cafés and restaurants, especially along High and Court Streets.

A Key Pass ($9 adults, $6 children) gives admission to the following four attractions, all within easy walking distance. At the water end of London Street, the retired Coast Guard vessel *Portsmouth* houses the **Lightship Museum** (757/393-8591, 10 A.M.–5 P.M. Tues.–Sat., 1–5 P.M. Sun., www.portsnavalmuseums.com, $3 adults, $1 children 2–17, admission includes Naval Shipyard Museum). Commissioned in 1915 and anchored offshore, the ship guided vessels into the tricky Hampton Roads harbor for decades before being restored as a floating museum and National Historic Landmark. Tour the captain's quarters, boiler room, and crew's mess.

Ship models, artifacts, and uniforms fill the **Naval Shipyard Museum** (757/393-8591, 10 A.M.–5 P.M. Tues.–Sat., 1–5 P.M. Sun., www.portsnavalmuseums.com, $3 adults, $1 children 2–17, admission includes Lightship Museum). The collection, dating to the 1700s, includes antique diving helmets.

A bubble-making station, rock-climbing wall, and an antique toy and model train collection to please Thomas the Tank Engine fans are only a few of the diversions at the **Children's Museum of Virginia** (221 High St., 757/393-5258, 9 A.M.–5 P.M. Tues.–Sat., 11 A.M.–5 P.M. Sun., www.childrensmuseum va.com, $5). In 2009, major renovations began to add 12,000 square feet and new exhibits, with the museum's reopening expected for early 2011. In the interim the museum has opened **Andalo's Clubhouse** at 420 High Street. It's next to the Courthouse Galleries and continues to focus on science, the arts, and fun.

Portsmouth's **Courthouse Galleries** (High and Court St., 757/393-8543, 9 A.M.–5 P.M. Tues.–Sat., 11–5 P.M. Sun., www.courthouse galleries.com, $5) fill a restored 1846 courthouse with works by international and regional artists.

Immerse yourself in the athletic world, from dribbling a basketball to driving a stock car on a (simulated) professional track, at the **Virginia Sports Hall of Fame & Museum** (206 High St., 757/393-8031, 10 A.M.–5 P.M. Mon.–Sat., 1–5 P.M. Sun. Memorial Day to Labor Day, shorter off-season hours, www .vshfm.com, $7).

Entertainment and Recreation

One of the best sound systems in Hampton Roads makes a movie at the **Commodore Theatre** (421 High St., 757/393-6962, www .commodoretheatre.com, $8) an experience not to be missed. Built in 1945, the art deco theater underwent a two-year $800,000 restoration that brought back 40-foot canvas murals and Italian lead crystal chandeliers. You can enjoy appetizers and light meals during the show in the 200-person dining area downstairs, but up in the balcony you'll have to be content with the usual movie snacks.

Lantern Tours of Olde Towne are led by a guide in period attire on Tuesday and Sunday evenings June–September (757/393-5111, $5). Check at the visitors center for information. Portsmouth's **Memorial Day Parade** is a big local event, and the oldest in the country.

Information

Portsmouth's **visitors center** is near the riverfront just past the corner of Crawford and High Streets (6 Crawford St., 757/393-5111, www.visitportsva.com, 9 A.M.–5 P.M. daily). For details on Portsmouth festivals and events, visit www.portsvaevents.com.

Getting There

Portsmouth is connected to Newport News, Hampton, Norfolk, Virginia Beach, and Chesapeake by **Hampton Roads Transit** (757/222-6100, www.gohrt.com). HRT also runs the **Paddlewheel Ferry,** leaving regularly from North Landing and High Street for Norfolk's Waterside daily for $1.50; call or see the website for a current schedule.

GREAT DISMAL SWAMP NATIONAL WILDLIFE REFUGE

Steeped in mystery, legend, and dread, this sodden corner of the state is actually more beautiful than it is dreary, and it still bursts with life despite multiple attempts to tame its wildness. Deep peat bogs echo with the strange cries of concealed animals down long, straight canals that contrast against the seething disorder of the bog.

History

Estimates put the age of the swamp at close to 10,000 years, when the rivers flowing through it began to slow and accumulate peat. An Indian legend of a great fireball falling from the sky has led some to believe that 3,100-acre Lake Drummond—one of only two natural lakes in the state—was formed by a meteorite. Early colonists saw the swamp as an ugly hindrance rather than a wildlife haven and tried their best to "improve" it. In 1728, after nearly losing his life surveying the state line, Col. William Byrd gave the area its name and called it a "vast body of dirt and nastiness [that] not even a Turkey Buzzard will venture to fly over."

George Washington organized a logging company in 1763, building roads and digging drainage ditches through what he considered a "glorious paradise." One 22-mile canal bearing his name is the oldest artificial waterway in the country. Eventually most of the timber was cut, leaving the swamp a shadow of its former self. In 1973, the Nature Conservancy transferred 49,100 acres to the Department of the Interior to make into a National Wildlife Refuge. Today, the Great Dismal Swamp covers over 112,000 acres in Virginia and North Carolina, primarily in Virginia.

Habitats and Residents

Ironically, human interference has left a greater variety of habitats than if the swamp had been left alone. Mixed forest, brier thickets, pine barrens, and shrub bogs now surround the original cypress swamps, whose peaty depths can reach 18 feet. Vines, including the tree-strangling supplejack, colorful hydrangea, and fast-growing Virginia creeper, festoon the branches of maples, black gums, and bald cypress, with their knobby mud-level "knees" and swollen lower trunks. Poison ivy vines as thick as your arm and a sharp-spined shrub called the devil's walking stick will make you want to hew to the trails. Venture out at night and you'll probably see the ghostly glow of foxfire (a type of fungus) in the distance. The swamp is home to declining bird species such as the bright yellow prothonotary warbler, and millions of blackbirds roost here in the winter.

In among the greenery live otters, raccoons, foxes, mink, and white-tailed deer, along with the rare bobcat and black bear. Snakes, including copperheads, rattlers, and cottonmouth moccasins, are all found here, albeit infrequently, as well as 22 species of amphibians and dozens of kinds of birds. The tannic acid is too much for most fish to live in Lake Drummond, whose position in an unusual "perched bog" makes it the highest point in the swamp.

Visiting the Swamp

One hundred forty miles of hiking and biking trails follow old drainage ditches from one end of the swamp to the other. Boating on Lake Drummond, accessed via a feeder ditch from the Dismal Swamp Canal, is also popular (there's a public boat ramp north of the feeder ditch). Bring water, good shoes, and above all insect repellent—the mosquitoes are merciless. Spring is the best time to catch migrating birds and the tiny blooms of dwarf trillium. The main **Washington Ditch entrance,** off Route 32 south of Suffolk via U.S. 13, is open sunrise to sunset daily year-round, and offers access to a one-mile **Boardwalk Trail** over the swamp. On this day-use path, you'll see bald cypress draped with Spanish moss standing over dark water. (The Jericho Lane entrance is open the same hours.) The 8.5-mile **Dismal Swamp Canal Trail,** once part of Route 17, is now a multiuse trail along the canal open to walkers, horseback riders, bicyclists, and boaters (who use it for water access, of course). Find the northern trailhead where Dominion Boulevard meets Old Route 17 in Chesapeake.

For more information, contact the refuge office in Suffolk (3100 Desert Rd., 757/986-3705, www.fws.gov/northeast/greatdismal swamp, 8 A.M.–4 P.M. Mon.–Fri.).

Virginia Beach and Vicinity

With 35 miles of beaches, surf, sand, and sun, Virginia's premier seaside resort has it all, along with gloriously tacky gift shops and more than 433,000 people in residence. While Virginia Beach has suffered an over-commercialized fate similar to places like Ocean City, Maryland, from the beach it's hard to question the pleasures of sunshine and crashing waves, no matter what's on the boardwalk behind you. And you can't argue with the variety: Be it miniature golf, family festivals, wide beaches, or a world-class aquarium, you can probably find it in Virginia Beach, although you might have to share it with a few thousand new friends.

Tourism, obviously, is one of the top local industries, ever since the first beachfront hotel went up in 1884. The boardwalk was built four years later, and the landmark Cavalier hotel arrived in 1927—both are still going strong. Virginia's most populous city didn't really become a national resort, though, until recently. The population doubled between 1980 and 1990, and it currently welcomes nearly three million visitors annually.

The municipality has invested hundreds

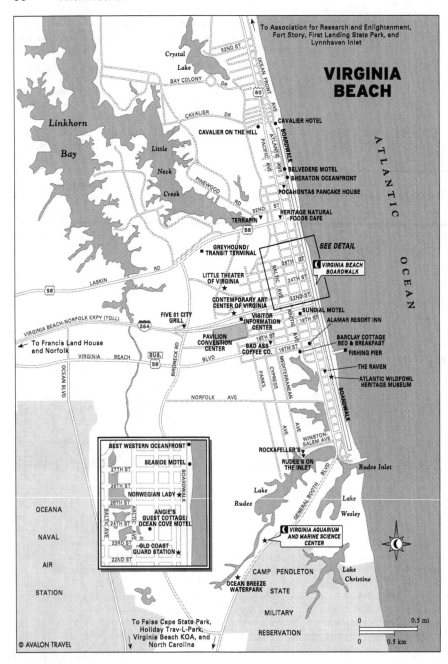

To Association for Research and Enlightenment,
Fort Story, First Landing State Park, and
Lynnhaven Inlet

VIRGINIA BEACH

Crystal Lake

BAY COLONY DR

52ND ST

OCEAN FRONT AVE

Linkhorn Bay

Little Neck Creek

CAVALIER DR

CAVALIER HOTEL

CAVALIER ON THE HILL

BOARDWALK

PACIFIC AVE

ATLANTIC AVE

BELVEDERE MOTEL
SHERATON OCEANFRONT

POCAHONTAS PANCAKE HOUSE

PINEWOOD RD

32ND ST

TERRAPIN

58

HERITAGE NATURAL FOODS CAFE

A T L A N T I C   O C E A N

GREYHOUND/ TRANSIT TERMINAL

LITTLE THEATER OF VIRGINIA

CONTEMPORARY ART CENTER OF VIRGINIA

SEE DETAIL

BALTIC AVE

28TH ST

24TH ST

22ND ST

VIRGINIA BEACH BOARDWALK

RD

LASKIN

58

FIVE 01 CITY GRILL

264

VISITOR INFORMATION CENTER

ARCTIC AVE

19TH ST

SUNDIAL MOTEL

ALAMAR RESORT INN

VIRGINIA BEACH-NORFOLK EXPY (TOLL)

To Francis Land House and Norfolk

VIRGINIA BEACH

BUS. 58

BIRDNECK RD

PAVILION CONVENTION CENTER BLVD

BAD ASS COFFEE CO.

16TH ST

MEDITERRANEAN AVE

BARCLAY COTTAGE BED & BREAKFAST

FISHING PIER

THE RAVEN

ATLANTIC WILDFOWL HERITAGE MUSEUM

OCEAN BLVD

NORFOLK AVE

CYPRESS AVE

PARKS AVE

BOARDWALK

WINSTON-SALEM AVE

ROCKAFELLER'S

RUDEE'S ON THE INLET

GENERAL BOOTH BLVD

Rudee Inlet

BEST WESTERN OCEANFRONT

SEASIDE MOTEL

27TH ST

26TH ST

25TH ST

24TH ST

23RD ST

22ND ST

BALTIC AVE

ARCTIC AVE

BOARDWALK

NORWEGIAN LADY

ANGIE'S GUEST COTTAGE/ OCEAN COVE MOTEL

OLD COAST GUARD STATION

Lake Rudee

Lake Wesley

VIRGINIA AQUARIUM AND MARINE SCIENCE CENTER

Lake Christine

OCEANA

NAVAL

AIR

STATION

CAMP PENDLETON

OCEAN BREEZE WATERPARK

STATE

MILITARY

RESERVATION

To False Cape State Park,
Holiday Trav-L-Park,
Virginia Beach KOA, and
North Carolina

0   0.5 mi

0   0.5 km

© AVALON TRAVEL

Richmond artist and sculptor Paul DiPasquale's statue of King Neptune greets you on the Virginia Beach boardwalk.

of millions of dollars to make its beachside resort area more welcoming and family oriented, from boutique shops to high-end hotels and restaurants to high-profile PR campaigns canvassing metropolises such as Washington, D.C., nearby. New benches and lighting, wider sidewalks, buried power lines, and a boardwalk bicycle trail have all transformed Pacific and Atlantic Avenues.

The effort seems to have paid off: The Clean Beaches Council has officially recognized Virginia Beach as a Blue Wave beach, for excellence in public safety and environmental health. Numerous awards for livability, mostly revolving around fitness—Best Walking City, Most Stroller-Friendly City, and so on—attest to the high value locals and visitors place on getting out and about. Further testimony to this sporty streak is the perennially popular Virginia Beach Rock 'n' Roll Half Marathon; more than 15,000 runners descend on the boardwalk for the Labor Day weekend race. Any time of year, navy jets roar overhead regularly, reminders of the strong military presence in Hampton Roads.

Orientation

The resort area of Virginia Beach stretches north and south along the main beach area, lined by the boardwalk from 1st Street through 42nd Street. This is where most of the hotels, restaurants, and tourist shops are, as well as the oceanfront amusement park. Locals call the beach from 43rd Street to 86th Street "the North End"—you can rent homes here at any time of year, and there are bike paths and a wide feeder road. Sandbridge, south of Camp Pendleton toward Back Bay, offers more seclusion and rustic beach homes for rent. Chick's Beach is a calm beach area along the bay north of the resort area that includes Lynnhaven Inlet. Here you can charter a boat for sportfishing and then pull right up to a dockside restaurant for dinner when you return.

SIGHTS
◖ Virginia Beach Boardwalk

Virginia Beach's pride and joy, a wide expanse of pure white sand facing the Atlantic, stretches along "the Strip" from 1st Street to 42nd Street. The city's sandy heart has been significantly spruced up by a $125 million erosion control and hurricane protection project. In 2001, the beach was widened by the length of a football field using 3.2 million cubic yards of imported sand—enough to fill 15,000 residential swimming pools. There are information kiosks open in the summer at 17th and 24th Streets, and public restrooms at 17th, 24th, and 30th Streets open year-round. You can rent beach umbrellas and chairs from vendors on the beach.

From Memorial Day through Labor Day, certified lifeguards are stationed every block 9:30 A.M.–6 P.M. daily (and at various stations along the beach until dusk), keeping an eye out for wayward vacationers and anyone drinking alcohol without a special-event permit. Surfing is allowed in designated areas on the north end and in Sandbridge, as well as in the main resort area during certain times (it's forbidden 10 A.M.–4 P.M. weekdays and to 6 P.M. weekends). Wave-riders congregate near Rudee Inlet and the 14th Street pier.

The **Norwegian Lady** faces the sea at 25th Street, where the bark *Dictator* sank in 1891. A twin of the nine-foot bronze figurehead stands in Moss, Norway, a sister city to Virginia Beach. The sand becomes less crowded as you head north into Fort Story or south to Croatan.

Disabled visitors can borrow all-terrain wheelchairs for free on the boardwalk (they'll lock up your standard wheelchair for you until you return; call 757/385-5659 for details). For more information on beach regulations, visit www.vbgov.com.

◖ Virginia Aquarium and Marine Science Center

You'll find yourself eye-to-eye with a harbor seal before you're even inside this place, the most popular aquarium in the state and one of the best of its kind in the country. From the seal pool at the entrance to a drift through a kelp forest in the three-dimensional IMAX theater, the aquarium draws 620,000 visitors per year (from the sound of it sometimes, mostly schoolchildren), with a collection that's the next best thing to strapping on a scuba tank and getting wet yourself.

More than 300 exhibits include aquariums galore containing more than 800,000 gallons of fresh and saltwater. Starting with the 300,000-gallon Norfolk Canyon Aquarium, these pools are the highlight of any visit. See if you can count five varieties of sharks, and don't miss the sea-turtle hatchling laboratory next to the aquarium holding the youngsters' cat-eyed

© KATIE GITHENS

It's easy to imagine yourself underwater while visiting the Virginia Aquarium.

parents. The Ray Touch Pool is full of harmless stingrays that are so eager to be petted that they pop halfway out of the water. Just down the hall are exhibits on deep-sea diving and beach ecology. Try your hand at oyster tonging before taking a walk down the nature trail to the marsh pavilion, where you can watch river otters cavorting and ospreys nesting on specially built platforms near their brethren enclosed in the outdoor aviary.

Be sure to visit Restless Planet, a multimillion-dollar 12,000-square-foot renovation that opened in 2009 and doubled the aquarium's animal collection, adding species that could surprise you—among them, Komodo dragons, cobras, and impossibly cute hedgehogs. The newest exhibit features four diverse habitats (a Malaysian peat swamp, coastal Sahara Desert, the Red Sea, and Indonesia's Flores Island) that resemble ecosystems that existed in Virginia millions of years ago, but are now only found in more remote corners of the globe.

The aquarium (717 General Booth Blvd., 757/385-3474, www.vmsm.com, 9 A.M.–5 P.M. daily, extended summer hours, $17 adults, $12 children 3–11) has various IMAX combination tickets available and also organizes various day trips.

Old Coast Guard Station

From 1875 to 1915, more than 600 ships foundered and sank off the Virginia coast, prompting the creation of 11 life-saving stations from the North Carolina border to the Eastern Shore. This 1903 building is the only one left of five along the southern Virginia shore. Formerly called the Life-Saving Museum, the Old Coast Guard Station (24th St. and Boardwalk, 757/422-1587, www.oldcoast guardstation.com, 10 A.M.–5 P.M. Mon.–Sat., noon–5 P.M. Sun., closed Mon. off-season, $4 adults, $2 children 6–18) still traces the history of early rescue efforts, which is really the history of Virginia Beach because the town grew up around the five nearby stations.

Among other exhibits, a roof-mounted "Towercam" allows guests to identify far-off ships, and the museum's archives hold over 1,800 photographs. Knowledgeable volunteers tell you how the attic is said to be haunted, ever since the bodies of wreck victims were stored there.

Atlantic Wildfowl Heritage Museum

The long history of bird hunting is told in the centuries-old DeWitt Cottage (1113 Atlantic Ave., 757/437-8432, www.awhm.org, 10 A.M.–5 P.M. Mon.–Sat., noon–5 P.M. Sun., closed Mon. off-season, free, donations welcome) in prints, decoys, and marvelously detailed sculptures.

Contemporary Art Center of Virginia

The only museum of its kind in the state, the Contemporary Art Center (2200 Parks Ave., 757/425-0000, www.cacv.org, 10 A.M.–5 P.M. Tues.–Fri., 10 A.M.–4 P.M. Sat., noon–4 P.M. Sun., $7 adults, $3 children 4–14) is a nonprofit institution founded in 1952. An airy main atrium filled with trees and windows leads to galleries full of paintings, sculptures, photographs, and works in glass, video, and other media. Studio art classes and outdoor shows are part of the schedule of regularly changing exhibits, which have included the likes of Maurice Sendak's *Where the Wild Things Are* illustrations.

Association for Research and Enlightenment (A.R.E.)

The work of Edgar Cayce, the 20th-century American psychic known as the father of holistic medicine, is the basis for this institution and museum. After entering a self-induced trance, Cayce would deliver predictions on the future and surprisingly accurate diagnoses of patients from just their names and addresses. Opened in 1931, the A.R.E. has some 14,000 transcripts of the sessions, called "readings," including the one that convinced Cayce to move to Virginia Beach and open the center. It's one of the largest metaphysical libraries in the world—second only to the Vatican.

The A.R.E. (67th St. and Atlantic Ave., 757/428-3588 or 800/333-4499, www.edgarcayce.org, 9 A.M.–8 P.M. Mon.–Sat.,

11 A.M.–8 P.M. Sun.) has a daily list of free activities including group meditations, extrasensory perception (ESP) classes, and lectures on Cayce's work. You'll have to pay extra for yoga, meditation instruction, and evening lectures. The **A.R.E. Health Services Center** next door offers massage, hydrotherapy, Reiki, and various other spa treatments.

Fort Story

In the middle of this U.S. Army base, north of the boardwalk on Atlantic Avenue, stands the **Battle Off the Capes Monument,** replacing one erected by Jamestown colonists under Capt. Christopher Newport on April 29, 1607, in gratitude for a safe arrival on solid ground. Part of Colonial National Historical Park, the memorial describes the naval battle that raged offshore on September 5, 1781, between 24 French ships commanded by Adm. Comte de Grasse and 19 British vessels under Rear Adm. Charles Graves. After surprising the French at anchor, the British hesitated long enough for the colonists' allies to line up in battle formation and win after a brief fight. Cornwallis was thus denied

© CINDY HAGGERTY / 123RF.COM

Old Cape Henry Lighthouse in Fort Story

reinforcements, and the American Revolution was brought one step closer to success.

The official symbol of Virginia Beach, the **Old Cape Henry Lighthouse** (757/422-9421, www.apva.org/capehenry, 10 A.M.–5 P.M. daily mid-Mar.–Oct., to 4 P.M. Nov.–mid-Mar., $4 adults, $2 children 3–12) was built in 1791, the first building authorized by the first Congress. Stones from the same quarry that supplied the U.S. Capitol, the White House, and Mount Vernon went into the 90-foot octagonal tower set on the tallest sand hill in the area. In use until 1881, the lighthouse is now open to the public. The ascent—up a steep spiral staircase, two ladders, and through a small hole in the floor of the upper room—is not for the weak of heart or wide of midsection, but the view from the top is outstanding.

Remember that all visitors over 16 years old must show valid ID at the security gates of Fort Story, as it's still an active military base.

First Landing State Park

The inner half of Cape Henry manages to hide 2,900 acres of dunes, marshes, and cypress forest within sight of Virginia Beach's seaside strip. It's the most visited state park in Virginia, drawing more than one million sightseers annually, yet it remains an amazingly unspoiled nugget of nature considering its location within the state's most populous city. It also happens to be where the first permanent English settlers landed in America before settling in Jamestown.

First Landing protects mostly maritime forest, one of the most endangered habitat types in the world. The park ranges from tidal cordgrass salt marshes to live oak and loblolly pine scrub atop 75-foot dunes—the highest point in this part of the state—and shelters prothonotary warblers (also called swamp canaries) and wading birds such as green herons. Spring peepers, bullfrogs, and kingfishers ply the tannin-browned waters of gothic flooded forests in the center, one of the northernmost stands of Spanish moss and bald cypress in North America.

Stop at the **visitors center,** off Seashore Drive (U.S. 60) at the west end of the park

© KATIE GITHENS

First Landing State Park is a nice place for a stroll.

(757/412-2300, www.dcr.virginia.gov/state_parks/fir.shtml, $4 weekdays, $5 weekends), for a map of 20 miles of **hiking** trails. The six-mile Cape Henry trail runs the length of the park and is popular with mountain bikers, and the Bald Cypress Nature Trail leads into the heart of the swamp. The park's **Chesapeake Bay Center,** developed in cooperation with the Virginia Aquarium and Marine Science Center, houses displays on the aquatic life of the region and its human history. At the **Cape Henry Memorial,** part of Colonial National Historical Park, a cross erected in 1935 marks the approximate spot where the Jamestown settlers first landed. This park can get crowded, especially with trail runners, so come early and on weekdays to avoid the herds—and bring insect repellent. Primitive campsites near this entrance are $24–30 (Mar.–Dec.) and require advance reservations in the summer and on weekends year-round. Two-bedroom cabins ($88–132) are also available. The gates are open 8 A.M.–dusk daily, and parking is free.

Mount Trashmore Park

This aptly named park, on your right as you drive on I-264 from Norfolk to Virginia Beach, is the first above-ground solid-waste landfill to become a municipal park. It's over 60 feet high and 800 feet long and covers 165 acres. You'd never guess that underneath two lakes and a skateboard park lie 650,000 tons of garbage. The park includes Kids' Cove, a huge nautical-themed playground designed by children.

Historic Houses

Virginia Beach's three historic homes are each a substantial drive from the Boardwalk area. The **Adam Thoroughgood House** (1636 Parish Rd., 757/460-7588, 9 A.M.–5 P.M. Tues.–Sat., $7.50 adults, $4 children) is a 17th-century English cottage built of brick and oyster-shell mortar. Formal gardens and four rooms of antiques reflect the English ancestry of its builder, whose grandfather had come to Virginia as an indentured servant around 1620. The house, one of the oldest brick homes in the country, is on the Lynnhaven River directly east of the intersection of Northampton Boulevard (U.S. 13) and Independence Boulevard (Rte. 225).

A modest but elegant example of early Virginia architecture, **Lynnhaven House** (4401 Wishart Rd., 757/460-7109, 10 A.M.–4 P.M. Tues.–Sun., $7.50 adults, $4 children) dates to 1725. Costumed interpreters give tours of the home and demonstrate 18th-century skills and crafts. It's east of Independence Boulevard and south of the Adam Thoroughgood House.

Period attire–clad interpreters also lead tours of the **Francis Land House** (3131 Virginia Beach Blvd., 757/385-5100, 9 A.M.–5 P.M. Tues.–Sat., $7.50 adults, $4 children), a 200-year-old plantation home built by a wealthy local planter.

ENTERTAINMENT
Nightlife
Beach towns always have hopping after-hours activities going on, and Virginia Beach is no exception. Summer crowds tend toward the young, tanned, and beautiful, but whatever your stripe, you'll probably be able to find some place that's your speed. If you'd like a bite to eat with your music, try a restaurant-nightclub such as **Hot Tuna Bar & Grill** (2817 Shore Dr., 757/481-2888, www.hottunavb.com).

The Jewish Mother (3108 Pacific Ave., 757/422-5430, www.jewishmother.com) is a bit of a dive but is a dependable live music spot, featuring jazz, folk, and blues most nights. It serves deli-style sandwiches to boot. You can catch acoustic performances at the **Abbey Road Restaurant** (203 22nd St., 757/425-6330, www.abbeyroadpub.com) and **Smackwater Jack's** (3333 Virginia Beach Blvd., 757/340-6638). **Peabody's** (209 21st St., 757/422-6212) has the biggest dance floor in town.

For a game of pool, stop by **Q-Master II Billiards** (5612 Princess Anne Rd., 757/499-8900, www.q-masters.com). For a chuckle, try the **Funny Bone Comedy Club & Restaurant** (217 Central Park Ave., 757/213-5555, www.vabeachfunnybone.com) at Town Center, which has hosted high-caliber comics such as Mark Curry and D. L. Hughley.

The **Verizon Wireless Virginia Beach Amphitheater** (3550 Cellar Door Way, 757/368-3000, www.vwvba.com) presents 40 or so concerts per season. Performers include the likes of John Mayer, Kenny Chesney, Aerosmith, and Sting. There's space for 12,500 people on the lawn in addition to 7,500 covered seats. It's off Princess Anne Road near Princess Anne Park.

Performing Arts
Not all of Virginia Beach's nighttime entertainment involves booze and shaking your booty. Both the **Virginia Beach Symphony Orchestra** (291 Independence Blvd., Ste. 421, 757/671-8611, www.symphonicity.org) and the **Virginia Beach Ballet** (4716 Larkspur Square Shopping Center, 757/495-0989) perform locally. The **Little Theater of Virginia Beach** (550 Barberton Dr. at 24th St., 757/428-9233, www.ltvb.com) showcases local thespian talent. These acts sometimes take to the stage at the Sandler Center for the Performing Arts (201 Market St., 757/385-2787, www.sandlercenter.org), which features local, regional, and national performing artists, with 1,200 seats and an outdoor performance plaza.

Virginia Beach has no shortage of outdoor venues. Six outdoor stages grace the boardwalk at 7th, 13th, 17th, 24th, 25th, and 31st Streets; contact Beach Street USA for details on free concerts and movies in the summer months (757/425-3111, www.beachstreetusa.com).

RECREATION
Fishing
A boatload of places offer half-day, full-day, and overnight **charters** in pursuit of the marlin, dolphin, tuna, rockfish (aka striped bass), tautog, sailfish, and wahoo that teem offshore at the right times of year. At Rudee Inlet, at the south end of Pacific Avenue at the bridge, the **Virginia Beach Fishing Center** (200 Winston-Salem Ave., 757/491-8000 or 800/725-0509, www.virginiafishing.com) runs half- and full-day on- and off-shore trips starting at $600. It also rents personal watercraft and offers parasailing.

If all you want is to get a hook in the water, you can rent rods, reels, and crab cages May–October at the **Virginia Beach Fishing Pier** (15th St. at Oceanfront, 757/428-2333), near the small amusement park, and the **Lynnhaven Fishing Pier** (2350 Starfish Rd. off Shore Dr., 757/481-7071). In November 2009 a wicked nor'easter knocked down portions of the Lynnhaven Pier, but through a fundraiser that sold boards for $100 apiece, it's scheduled to reopen in May 2010. Look for the new wooden planks engraved with the names of donors who helped to restore the local landmark. No fishing license is required at the piers, but you do have to pay a small entrance fee.

Scuba Diving

Explore centuries of shipwrecks for $75–150 per dive ($350 for overnighters) with the **Lynnhaven Dive Center** (1413 N. Great Neck Rd., 757/481-7949, www.ldcscuba.com), which offers certification courses in its heated indoor pool. Visibility is usually 40–50 feet, and many wrecks have some coral growth.

Surfing

When James Jordan stood up on a 110-pound redwood board off Virginia Beach around 1912, he became the first person to surf the East Coast. Virginia Beach is now home to the East Coast Surfing Championships, North America's oldest running surfing competition, held each summer. For board sales, rentals, and advice, try the **17th Street Surf Shop** (1612 Pacific Ave., 757/422-6105, www.17thstsurfshop.com). **Ocean Rentals** (577 Sandbridge Rd., 757/721-6210, www.oceanrentalsltd.com) also offers surfboard rentals and lessons for all ages and experience levels. Former East Coast surf champion Jason Borte teaches surfing at the **Billabong Surf Camp** (757/965-9659, www.thesurfschool.com).

Natural History Excursions

Guided kayak tours on Virginia Beach's 120 miles of waterways are only one way to get up close and personal with the amazing variety of life in the surrounding ecosystems. Dolphin kayak trips start at $49 per person for three hours with outfits like **Wild River Outfitters** (3636 Virginia Beach Blvd., Ste. 108, 757/431-8566, www.wildriveroutfitters.com) and **Kayak Nature Tours** (757/480-1999 or 888/669-8368, www.tidewateradventures.com). They both also offer sunset and overnight trips and paddling instruction, and the latter rents kayaks.

The **Virginia Aquarium and Marine Science Center** (717 General Booth Blvd., 757/385-3474, www.vmsm.com) offers 90-minute and two-hour trips year-round that explore different facets of Virginia Beach's rich waters. Whale-watching excursions (Dec.–Mar., $28 adults, $24 children) go after humpbacks and fin whales with cameras instead of harpoons. In spring and summer, the mid-Atlantic's largest population of bottlenose dolphins can often be seen offshore on the museum's dolphin-watching trips (Apr.–Oct., $19 adults, $14 children). Check the city's visitors website (www.vbfun.com) for a list of operators offering dolphin-watching trips, which run 1–2 hours.

Chesapean Outdoors (313 Laskin Rd., 757/961-0447, www.chesapean.com) is an eco-tour company that offers guided dolphin tours in the summer months ($55 pp), along with kayaking, surfing, fishing, and sailing charters. **Back Bay Getaways** (3713 S. Sandpiper Rd., 757/721-4484, www.backbaygetaways.com) runs guided kayak and mountain bike tours at the southern end of Sandbridge Beach.

Other Activities

The three-mile bike trail along the boardwalk will make you glad you brought your wheels or soon have you looking for some to rent. **Cherie's Bicycle and Blade Rentals** (757/437-8888, www.cheriesbikes.com) rents bikes, in-line skates, and safety gear from its 12 locations along the boardwalk. Innumerable beach-supply places also rent bikes and in-line skates along with boogie boards, beach chairs, strollers, and umbrellas. Try your hand (and heart) at parasailing in the one- and two-person Skyriders operated by the **Virginia Beach Fishing Center.**

The **Ocean Breeze Waterpark** (849 General Booth Blvd., 757/422-4444, www.oceanbreezewaterpark.com, daily Memorial Day–Labor Day, $24 adults, $17 children under 10) has a million-gallon wave pool, water flume, and 16 slides. You'll have to buy individual passes for miniature golf, batting cages, and rides such as the Grand Prix cars in Motorworld Thrill Park.

Another popular (and free) diversion in Virginia Beach is to watch **navy jets** take off from the Oceana Naval Air Station along Oceana Boulevard and London Bridge Road. There's an observation park at the POW/MIA Memorial Park on Oceana Boulevard, near the F/A18 Super Hornet runways. Tours of the base are available from early June through August. Call 757/433-3131 for a schedule and details.

SHOPPING

If your tastes don't run to seashell fishermen and sunset ashtrays, a few places in town sell souvenirs of a more memorable kind. **Echoes of Time** (600 N. Witchduck Rd., 757/428-2332, www.echoes-of-time.com) offers vintage clothing and books, along with well-used furniture.

At the corner of Dam Neck and Princess Anne Roads, the **Virginia Beach Farmers Market** (3640 Dam Neck Rd., 757/385-4395, www.vbgov.com/farmersmarket) is open year-round with a litany of shops that sounds like a nursery rhyme: the grocer, the dairy, the butcher, the baker, the candy maker. Farmers sell produce in the partially enclosed public market during the growing season, and most merchants are open 10 A.M.–5 P.M. Monday–Saturday, noon–4 P.M. Sunday.

EVENTS

Most Virginia Beach festivals involve music or sports in proximity to the ocean. For more information, contact the visitors center or **Beach Street USA** (757/425-3111, www.beachstreet usa.com).

In April, the **Atlantic Coast Kite Festival** takes flight on the beach between 16th and 18th Streets. Early summer brings several options: in **Monsters on the Beach,** cult-classic monster trucks like Grave Digger and Monster Mutt do battle on the sand; **Beach Music Weekend** in mid-May has performances on the 29th Street stages; and bring your *djembe* for the drum circles at the **World Music Drum Festival** at 17th Street Park in late May.

In early June, the **North American Sand Soccer Championships** (www.sandsoccer .com) are sponsored by the Hampton Roads Soccer Council. They are followed by the **Boardwalk Art Show and Festival** (www .cacv.org), held since 1955, between 17th and 32nd Streets along the beach. That same month the sounds of merengue and mambo mingle with the smells of spicy cuisine and vibrant works of art during the **Latin Fest.**

In July, the **Mid-Atlantic Hermit Crab Challenge** begins with a Most Curvaceous Crustacean pageant and continues with racing heats that culminate in the championship Crustacean 500 race. The fastest hermit crab scuttles away with the coveted Order of the Mercury Claw trophy.

Since 1963, the **East Coast Surfing Championships** (www.surfecsc.com) have determined the best North Atlantic rider in professional and amateur categories. Held in August, the second-oldest continuously run surfing competition in the world draws hundreds of surfers and viewers with live music, a 5K race, and volleyball, skateboarding, and swimsuit competitions. The **Verizon Wireless American Music Festival** in early September welcomes 30 bands, including national acts from pop to country. Performances are held along the oceanfront from 5th to 31st Streets. Labor Day weekend kicks off the **Virginia Beach Rock 'n' Roll Half Marathon** (800/311-1255, www.virginia-beach.competitor.com).

September also brings Virginia Beach's biggest blowout, the **Neptune Festival** (www .neptunefestival.com). Parades, surfing, sailing, and the North American Sand Sculpting Competitions alternate with the Sandman Triathlon, a U.S. Navy Air Show, and the formal King Neptune's Ball. The **Oktober Brewfest,** held in the 24th Street park, celebrates all things German with food, drink, oompah bands, and a dachshund beauty pageant. From mid-November through the end of

VIRGINIA BEACH AND VICINITY   **69**

December, the boardwalk is illuminated with surfing Santas and glowing sea creatures during **Holiday Lights at the Beach,** with over half a million sparkling lights. (It's the only time you're allowed to drive on the boardwalk.) Virginia Beach's historic homes are also decorated around the holidays, and play host to candlelit tours, tavern nights, and Yule log celebrations.

Various fishing tournaments are held throughout the year, including the **Virginia Saltwater Fishing Tournament** year-round and the **Virginia Beach Billfish Tournament** in August.

ACCOMMODATIONS

At last count, some 12,000 rooms, 1,800 campsites, and hundreds of rental cottages were available in Virginia Beach. Many offer bay or ocean views. Keep in mind that rates can vary wildly from one season to the next. High season is loosely defined as May to mid-September, plus a week in March for spring break. From November to February or March is the low season, leaving March–May and September–November in between. The same room can cost three times as much in June as it does in January. (Prices listed here are for high season.)

Many hotels require a minimum stay and offer good deals midweek and during shoulder season. Call the visitors center for help finding accommodations.

Under $100

Angie's Guest Cottage (302 24th St., 757/491-1830, www.angiescottage.com) is a comfy house in the center of the strip with six air-conditioned private rooms for $65–100. Angie's HI-USA Hostel (Apr.–Oct.) has five dorm-style rooms with a total of 34 bunk beds for $20–32 per bed per night. There's a porch, library, and full kitchen.

Most of the rooms at the **Seaside Motel** (2705 Atlantic Ave., 757/428-9341 or 800/348-7263, www.seasidehotel.net) are in this price range, and some are efficiencies. There's a sun deck and a heated indoor pool.

$100-150

Next door to Angie's and under the same management is the **Ocean Cove Motel** (300 24th St., 757/491-1830, www.oceancovemotel.com), with three-bedroom, two-bath cottages. Call for daily rates, though in summer season reservations are only taken for weekly bookings ($950–1,350/week). Also in this price range is the **Belvedere Motel** (3603 Atlantic Ave., 757/425-0612), which offers good rates for being right on the ocean: $100–156 in season, along with an outdoor pool and bicycles for guests.

The **Alamar Resort Inn** (311 16th St., 757/428-7582 or 800/346-5681, www.alamar resortinn.net) has 22 units (half one-bedroom, half suites with kitchens) set around a courtyard and heated pool for $72–210 in season. Sixty-seven rooms (half efficiencies) at the **Sundial Motel & Efficiencies** (308 21st St., 757/428-2922, www.sundialvirginiabeach .com) run $50–230.

$150-250

Opened in 1927, the original **⟨ Cavalier Hotel** (42nd St. at Oceanfront, 757/425-8555 or 800/446-8199, www.cavalierhotel.com) was *the* place to stay in Virginia Beach between the wars. Chauffeured limos and Pullman coaches brought seven presidents and celebrities including Jean Harlow, Fatty Arbuckle, and Johnny Weissmuller (Olympic swimmer and the original Tarzan) to enjoy the indoor seawater pool and swing at the Cavalier Beach Club. During the 1930s, 1940s, and 1950s it was the largest booker of big bands in the world; everyone from Frank Sinatra to Glenn Miller played at the Cavalier Beach Club. The hotel on the hill became a radar training school in the 1940s. Today it has undergone renovations and is open May–September, with rooms for $100–230. Suites are also available.

The newer **Cavalier Oceanfront,** open year-round, sits across Pacific Avenue on the beach. Guests can dine at tables favored by presidents in the Hunt Room. Guests can enjoy two Olympic-size pools, two clay tennis courts, shuffleboard, and a croquet lawn. The Cavalier Oceanfront has a health club and Camp Cavalier for kids. Rooms for the Cavalier, both the original and the newer hotel, range $180–480 in season. Contact information is the same for both.

An 1895 summer cottage, one of Virginia Beach's more distinguished houses, has become the **Barclay Cottage Bed & Breakfast** (400 16th St., 757/422-1956 or 866/466-1895, www.barclaycottage.com). It once served as a boarding school where Ms. Lillian Barclay taught until age 80. Double-covered balconies run all the way around the building, decorated with antiques such as an 1810 sleigh bed and items donated by former students. It's open year-round, with five rooms (two with shared bathrooms) for $155–225.

At the two-part **Best Western Oceanfront** (2809 Atlantic Ave., 757/428-5370 or 800/344-3342, www.col-inn.com), rates range $100–225 for oceanfront accommodations and slightly less for other rooms.

The **Sheraton Oceanfront** (3501 Atlantic Ave., 757/425-9000, www.sheratonvirginia beach.com) has close to 200 rooms right on the beach, along with two outdoor pools (one with a swim-up bar) and the Mediterranean-themed Aqua Vi restaurant. Rooms start around $200 in season.

Long-Term Rentals

Usually rented by the week, fully furnished houses and condominiums offer a comfortable alternative for extended stays. Prices range $700–2,200 per week during peak season for a two-bedroom apartment with full bath, kitchen, and dining room near the beach, with lower off-season rates. As an example, **Oceanfront Rentals** (314 26th St., 757/428-7473, www.oceanfrontrentals.homestead.com) has accommodations with one ($1,050 per week), two ($1,200), three ($1,775–1,995), or four bedrooms ($1,995–2,395). Virginia Beach Convention & Visitors Bureau has many more listings (www.vbfun.com).

For more information and options on vacation house rentals, contact **Siebert Realty** (601 Sandbridge Rd., 757/426-6200 or 877/422-2200, www.siebertrealty.com) or **Atkinson Realty** (5307 Atlantic Ave., 757/428-4441, www.atkinsonrealty.com).

Camping

The **Holiday Trav-L-Park** (1075 General Booth Blvd., 757/425-0249 or 866/849-8860, www.campingvb.com, open year-round) is the size of a small city, with more than 800 sites, four pools, sports courts, a restaurant, a miniature golf course, and a one-acre fenced dog park. Campsites are $39–77, and 44 cabins are $80–95.

Just down the road, the **Virginia Beach KOA** (1240 General Booth Blvd., 757/428-1444 or 800/562-4150, www.koavirginiabeach.com) has nearly 500 sites for $45–75 and cabins for $75–200. Campsites are also available in First Landing State Park. Primitive campsites are $24–30 (Mar.–Dec.) and require advance reservations in the summer and on weekends year-round. Two-bedroom cabins ($88–132) are also available.

FOOD

As you might expect, Virginia Beach has plenty of places to eat, with seafood spots leading the pack (about 300 at last count). Many restaurants add gratuities automatically—ask or check your bill.

Snacks and Cafés

Bad Ass Coffee Co. (619 18th St., 757/233-4007, breakfast and lunch daily) will kick-start your day with Kona coffee in a Hawaiian-style coffee shop near the oceanfront.

The **Pocahontas Pancake House** (Atlantic Ave. and 35th St., 757/428-6352) serves breakfast and lunch daily in its kitschy dining hall with wall-to-wall murals of Pocahontas, Capt. John Smith, and crew. Besides a dozen kinds of pancakes, you'll find Belgian waffles, French toast, and omelets galore. The **Heritage Natural Foods Cafe** (314 Laskin Rd., 757/428-0500, late breakfast and lunch daily) specializes in vegetarian entrées, sandwiches, and organic salads next to a natural foods market and New Age bookstore.

Casual

The Raven (Atlantic Ave. at 12th St., 757/425-1200, lunch and dinner daily) pulls off the usual beach-strip steaks, seafood, and poultry ($6–24) with a little more friendly flair than most.

An urban chic pervades the **Five 01 City Grill** (501 N. Birdneck, 757/425-7195, dinner daily) in the Birdneck Shoppes. Try the Southwest tuna tacos or trademark Michelob shrimp appetizers for around $10, followed by a Cajun bourbon penne pasta, pizza from the wood oven, or grilled rib-eye steak ($14–26), with a cappuccino or something from the long wine list to top it off.

In a big old three-story house on Rudee Inlet, **Rockafeller's** (308 Mediterranean Ave., 757/442-5654, lunch and dinner daily) is one of Virginia Beach's most popular standbys. Sit inside or out on two levels of covered balcony seating, it doesn't matter—the Caesar salads, crab cakes, steaks, and pasta are dependable favorites. Entrées range $15–30, but less expensive early-bird specials, kids' plates, and a moderately priced Sunday brunch are also offered. **Rudee's on the Inlet** (227 Mediterranean Ave., 757/425-1777, lunch and dinner daily, $15–30) is another popular choice nearby for fresh seafood, with a raw bar, an outdoor deck, and the requisite nautical decor.

Near the southern end of the Chesapeake Bay Bridge-Tunnel is **Alexander's on the Bay** (4536 Ocean View Ave., 757/464-4999, dinner daily), with fine dining in a weathered-wood setting or on an open-air beach deck. Escargot and baked brie appetizers ($8–11) lead to lobster, duck, and steak as well as pasta entrées for $18–32.

If the Mediterranean-style fresh fish of the day is any indication, the **Lynnhaven Fish House** (2350 Starfish Rd., 757/481-0003, lunch and dinner daily) serves seafood as good as any in Virginia Beach in front of picture windows overlooking the oceanfront. They claim to boast the largest fresh fish selection in Hampton Roads, with dinner entrées ($14–40) such as Chesapeake Bay crabs and pan-roasted mahimahi. Lunch dishes like seafood omelets, sandwiches, and quiches start at $8.

The best sushi in town belongs to **Kyushu Japanese Restaurant** (400 Newton Rd., 757/490-1177, lunch Mon.–Fri., dinner Mon.–Sat.), with rolls starting at $3.50 and various sushi and sashimi platters ranging $7.50–18. Traditional Japanese dishes like *yakisoba* (noodles sautéed with vegetables) and beef teriyaki are also on the menu.

For a switch from seafood, try **Jade Villa** (353 Independence Blvd., 757/473-2228, dinner daily, lunch and dim sum Sat.–Sun.), whose weekend dim sum selection, available 11 A.M.–2 P.M., comes highly recommended. Entrees range $9 to more than $20 for seafood and whole fish specials.

Upscale

Oddly enough, a number of fine-dining establishments in Hampton Roads are located in unassuming strip malls—so in this region especially you can't judge a restaurant by its storefront. Leading this argument is the **Cobalt Grille** (1624 Laskin Rd., Ste. 762, 757/333-3334, lunch and dinner Mon.–Sat.), located in the Hilltop North Shopping Center. English-born, Jamaican-bred chef Alvin Williams infuses many flavors into his contemporary American dishes, evident in the chicken penne pasta with sliced leeks and shallots. New York strip and Chesapeake jumbo lump crab cakes make it onto the menu both as entrées ($18–30) and tapas ($7.50–12), a choice at the trendy bar.

One Fish Two Fish (2109 W. Great Neck Rd., 757/496-4350, dinner daily) near the Lynnhaven Inlet bills itself as "upscale without the uppity," and this energetic waterside place feels like California with its open-air patio and exhibition kitchen. The seafood is imaginatively prepared (entrées $23–32), and the wine list is excellent.

◖ Coastal Grill (1427 N. Great Neck Rd., 757/496-3348, dinner daily) is arguably the most consistent gourmet meal in Virginia Beach, and has been since it opened its doors in 1989. Seafood is delicious here, but so are the lamb chops served in a cilantro sauce with a side of the restaurant's signature acorn squash basted in butter and brown sugar (entrées $17–24). They go through 600 bushels of squash each year! Live music, like classical guitar strummed in the corner, adds atmosphere to the cozy 65-seat restaurant on Sunday, Monday, and Wednesday evenings. Reservations recommended.

Three blocks away from the boardwalk, **◖ Terrapin** (3102 Holly Rd., 757/321-6688, dinner Tues.–Sun.) is the current Virginia Beach mecca for a special occasion meal. From truffle mac-and-cheese to martinis at the zebrawood bar, this fine-dining establishment strikes the right balance between classy and comfortable, and chef Rodney Einhorn continues to draw praise for his creative dishes. Farm-fresh ingredients, many of them organic, go into dinner entrées such as beef tenderloin with truffle carrot purée and pan-roasted rockfish with Israeli couscous ($18–38).

INFORMATION

The **Virginia Beach Visitors Center** (2100 Parks Ave., 757/437-4888 or 800/822-3224, www.vbfun.com, 9 A.M.–7 P.M. daily Memorial Day to Labor Day, to 5 P.M. rest of year) is near 21st Street. There are information kiosks along Atlantic Avenue at 17th and 24th Streets.

GETTING THERE AND AROUND
Getting There

Greyhound/Trailways has a terminal at 1017 Laskin Road (757/422-2998 or 800/231-2222). The nearest **Amtrak** station is in Newport News. A Thruway bus connects the terminal to the Amtrak shelter at 19th Street and Pacific Avenue.

If you're driving to North Carolina, try this neat route: Take Pacific Avenue south to Princess Anne Road (Rte. 615), which ends at Knott's Island at the southern end of Back Bay. From here a car ferry heads to Currituck, North Carolina. Call the North Carolina Department of Transportation Ferry Information Line (800/293-3779, www.ncdot.org/ferry) for up-to-the-minute ferry information.

Getting Around

Virginia Beach is connected to Newport News, Hampton, Norfolk, Portsmouth, and Chesapeake by **Hampton Roads Transit** (757/222-6100, www.gohrt.com). Call or check the website for routes, hours, and fares to these cities. **VB Wave Trolleys** run up and down Atlantic Avenue every 15 minutes 8 A.M.–2 A.M. daily May–September on route 30. The connecting Aquarium & Campground Shuttle (route 31) runs to the Virginia Aquarium and Marine Science Center, and the Shoppers' Shuttle (route 32) heads to the Hilltop area and the Lynnhaven Mall hourly 8 A.M.–2 A.M. Fares are $1.50 for adults (kids under 38 inches ride free), or you can buy five-day passes ($10).

BACK BAY NATIONAL WILDLIFE REFUGE

A thin strip of shoreline and a set of islands in Back Bay make up this sanctuary, which preserves 9,000 unspoiled acres of Virginia's southern Atlantic coast as it was before the high-rises and personal watercraft arrived. Once the haunt of wealthy duck hunters from New England, Back Bay National Wildlife Refuge was established in 1938 as an important stop along the Atlantic Flyway for migrating waterbirds, especially greater snow geese. Some 10,000 of these birds visit during their fall migration, usually around December.

A wide range of habitats starts among the sea oats on the mile-wide Atlantic strip, a constantly shifting stretch of sand that is predicted to eventually break free from the northern headland near Sandbridge. Maritime forests of scrub oak and loblolly pine cover the higher elevations, interspersed with wax myrtle shrubs and bayberry and blueberry bushes.

Three-quarters of the refuge is marsh, covering the bay side of the strip and Long and Ragged Islands at the north end of Back Bay.

Three hundred species of birds sighted here includes 30 kinds of waterfowl, among them the bald eagle and peregrine falcon. Spring is the peak migration time of songbirds and shorebirds, while hawks arrive in the fall. Tens of thousands of greater snow geese swing through November–March on their way south from Greenland and Canada's Northwest Territories. Snow goose migration peaks in December, accompanied by Canada geese and tundra swans. The mammal list includes gray foxes, river otters, mink, muskrats, and nutria (a large rodent), which compete with feral horses and pigs introduced by settlers. Back Bay is also one of the northernmost nesting spots for endangered loggerhead sea turtles, who drag themselves ashore in the summer to lay clutches of leathery eggs under the watchful eyes of refuge staff.

Visiting Back Bay

Take Sandbridge Road south to reach the entrance gate, open dawn–dusk daily ($5 per car or $2 per hiker). A **visitors center** (8 a.m.–4 p.m. Mon.–Fri., from 9 a.m. Sat.–Sun., closed Sat. Dec.–Mar.) has displays and films on the ecology of the refuge. Boardwalk trails cross the beach, while others along interior dikes are open to mountain bikes. Surf and freshwater fishing is permitted from land or small boats, which many visitors use to explore the bay and islands.

Camping is permitted only in False Cape State Park to the south, reached by a five-mile hike after parking outside the refuge gate. The fat-tire **Terra-Gator** (800/933-7275; reservations required), designed for minimal beach impact, runs to False Cape State Park through the refuge on weekends November–March ($8 pp, minimum 10 people). December and January are the best times to go to see peregrine falcons and bald eagles. The **Back Bay Restoration**

Foundation (757/721-7666, www.bbrf.org) runs three-hour guided **tram rides** through Back Bay and False Cape daily Memorial Day–Labor Day, and on a limited schedule the rest of the year, for $8 adults, $6 children under 12. For more information on Back Bay, contact the refuge office in Virginia Beach (757/721-2412, www.fws.gov/backbay).

FALSE CAPE STATE PARK

This mile-wide park—the least visited in the state—encloses six miles of pristine beaches, shore forest, and marsh at the primitive southern end of a barrier spit between the ocean and Back Bay. It earned its name—and its reputation as a ship graveyard—because 19th-century sea captains commonly confused it with Cape Henry at the entrance to the Chesapeake Bay. Halfway down lie the brick foundations and old cemetery of the town of Wash Woods, moved because of shifting dunes that threatened to inundate it. False Cape is home to an abundance of wildlife, including 54 rare and endangered species.

False Cape State Park prohibits private vehicles, so the general public can reach the park only by a six-mile hike or bike ride though Back Bay National Wildlife Refuge, via the tram through Back Bay National Wildlife Refuge, or by boat. Primitive **camping** is $11 per night. During the winter, the entrance may be closed; check with the **park office** (4001 Sandpiper Rd., Virginia Beach, 757/426-7128, www.dcr.virginia.gov/state_parks/fal.shtml) for details and information on various guided hikes and programs. The fat-tire **Terra-Gator** runs to False Cape State Park through the Back Bay National Wildlife Refuge on weekends November–March ($8 pp, minimum 10 people). It usually departs Little Island City Park in Virginia Beach at 9 a.m. and returns at 1 p.m.; reservations are required by calling 800/933-7275. This is the same number you should call for permits and information on using the 12 primitive campsites.

The Eastern Shore

"Junk & Good Stuff" reads a sign outside a store on U.S. 13, inadvertently but rather neatly summing up Virginia's Eastern Shore. The long, flat neck of the Delmarva Peninsula, dividing the Chesapeake Bay from the Atlantic from Maryland to Cape Charles, is something of a throwback, an often-forgotten corner of crusty watermen, rusty pickups, and salt breezes. It's also one of the most subtly enticing parts of Virginia.

They say that when you cross the Chesapeake Bay Bridge-Tunnel from Virginia Beach you step back in time, and it's not all hyperbole. A rural 1950s feeling pervades all 70 miles of the Eastern Shore, so after a while it's the modern cars on U.S. 13 that start to look out of place, not the vine-covered buildings slowly being reclaimed by the earth on either side. Fewer than 50,000 residents—more than in Charlottesville, fewer than in Lynchburg—are divided into "born-heres" (occasionally "stuck-heres") and recently arrived "come-heres," many of whom have opened bed-and-breakfasts in small historic towns.

Agriculture is the biggest money-maker on this peninsula, and most of the low-lying fields are covered with acres of potatoes, soy beans, and other crops. Seafood comes next, from netfuls of finfish to oyster beds and crab pots seeded the length of the bay. Pockets of poverty evidence the recent slipping of both industries.

Visiting the Eastern Shore

A slower pace of life means that it might take a little longer to get your crab cakes on the table, but use the time to savor your surroundings. Roadside stands selling produce, shrimp, fireworks, and flowers line U.S. 13, running the length of the Eastern Shore along a historic railroad route. (Route 600, running parallel, is a good back-road alternative.) Countless "creeks"—wide, shallow estuaries—perforate the "bayside" and "seaside," just waiting to be explored by boat. A few public beaches on the bay and ocean are open for swimming and fishing, and trails through miles of marshland are gold mines for bird-watchers.

Fans of historic architecture will have a field day with hundreds of buildings in continual use since before the Civil War. Many fit the classic country-house design of the 19th century, consisting of four connected structures—"big house," "little house," "colonnade," and "kitchen"—with a roofline like a descending bar graph. Towns like Eastville, Accomac, and Cape Charles brim with centuries-old churches, courthouses, schools, and homes.

Local transportation is provided by **Star Transit** (757/787-7332, www.mystartransit.com), whose bus routes run from Cape Charles to Chincoteague every few hours from early morning to midafternoon, Monday–Friday. Fares are $1.50–3, and the buses have bike racks and wheelchair ramps.

For more information on the Eastern Shore, contact the **Eastern Shore of Virginia Chamber of Commerce** (757/787-2460, www.esvachamber.org), which runs a visitors center on U.S. 13 just south of Melfa (19056 Industrial Pkwy., 8:30 A.M.–5 P.M. Mon.–Fri.). **Eastern Shore of Virginia Tourism** (757/787-8246, www.esvatourism.org) is another helpful organization.

EASTERN SHORE OF VIRGINIA NATIONAL WILDLIFE REFUGE

The southernmost tip of the Eastern Shore was set aside in 1984 as a sanctuary for migratory birds. Most of the 1,220 protected acres are saltwater marsh, with some maritime forest, grasslands, and thickets of myrtle and bayberry. The refuge includes most of Fisherman Island, the northernmost island crossed by the Chesapeake Bay Bridge-Tunnel, as well as Skidmore Island to the east.

Bird-watching is excellent from late August to early November due to the "funneling effect" that occurs as birds migrate down the Delmarva Peninsula and gather to wait until wind and weather conditions are right to cross the bay. Shorebirds including cattle egrets,

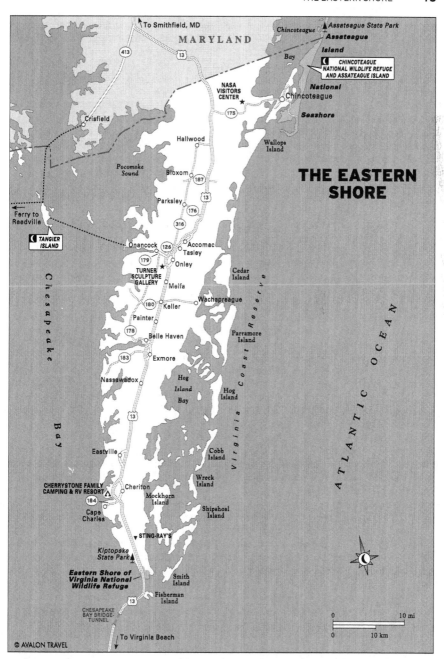

THE EASTERN SHORE

© AVALON TRAVEL

glossy ibis, and willets pass through in the spring, but the major migration takes place from late summer to early fall, when large groups of songbirds and raptors wait at the south side of the bay until weather conditions permit a crossing. Ospreys nest on special platforms in the spring and fall, and in the winter you have a good chance of spotting American kestrels, northern harriers, and snow geese. Bird species resident year-round include great blue herons, great horned owls, woodpeckers, and black ducks.

The refuge **visitors center** (9 A.M.–4 P.M. daily Apr.–Nov., reduced hours off-season) is beyond the northern end of the bridge. It has hands-on displays on the refuge's natural history and a viewing room over a marsh complete with binoculars and spotting scopes. A half-mile interpretive loop trail passes a 60-foot observation tower and old concrete gun emplacements that protected Norfolk's Naval Base during World War II. You can canoe or hike on your own from dawn to dusk, and free half-day guided tours of **Fisherman Island** leave Saturday mornings October–March (reservations required). Kayakers and canoeists can launch from the neighboring county boat ramp during daylight hours year-round. During the winter, staff lead tours on Fisherman Island (reservations also required). Contact the U.S. Fish and Wildlife Service in Cape Charles (5003 Hallett Circle, 757/331-2760, http://easternshore.fws.gov) for more information.

KIPTOPEKE STATE PARK

One of the few public beaches on the Eastern Shore started out as the northern terminus of the ferry to Virginia Beach, which moved to Cape Charles in 1949. Kiptopeke, which means "Big Water" in the Accawmack Indian language, now protects a half mile of sand with a swimming beach Memorial Day to Labor Day, as well as trails, a fishing pier, a boat launching ramp, and a full-service campground. Entrance is $4 per car on weekends ($3 weekdays), and naturalist programs are offered during the summer.

In addition to the 147 campsites ($24–35),

guests can rent a bunkhouse that sleeps 14 (call for rates), one of seven RV trailers (each sleeps six people), or a wood-frame yurt (sleeps six). The trailers cost $88–98 per night and are available March–November. It's the same pricing for the yurt, but it's only available until Labor Day. Five lodges were added in 2007, with full cooking and sleeping facilities and room for up to 16 people. They're open year-round for $249–371 per night. In general, the park requires a two-night stay minimum; in high season, Memorial Day through Labor Day, it's often a week.

The Virginia Society of Ornithology maintains a bird-banding station and raised observation platform to take advantage of the park's location on the Atlantic Flyway. Some 80,000 raptors pass through in early September and October, including sharp-shinned and Cooper's hawks, ospreys, bald eagles, and peregrine falcons. Kiptopeke's hawk observatory is considered one of the best in the country. The tours, presentations, and workshops of the **Eastern Shore Birding Festival** (757/787-2460) coincide with the peak fall migration in early October. Contact the park office in Cape Charles (757/331-2267, www.dcr.virginia.gov/state_parks/kip.shtml) for information on guided canoe tours through the park's marshes during the hawk migration.

CAPE CHARLES

This quiet town sprang up in 1884 as the southern terminus for the New York, Philadelphia, and Norfolk Railroad. Ferries carried automobiles and freight trains across the Chesapeake Bay to Norfolk and Hampton until the 1950s, when the freight business faded and the newly opened Chesapeake Bay Bridge-Tunnel killed the auto ferry. Today Cape Charles offers only hints that it was once the busiest town on the Eastern Shore, but its appeal hasn't faded completely.

Most of Cape Charles is a historic district. With more than 500 buildings erected between 1885 and 1940, this is one of the largest collections on the East Coast. Colonial Revival, neoclassic, and Victorian homes decorated with gingerbread woodwork line residential streets named after famous Virginians, fruits, and trees. Keep an eye out for several Sears Roebuck mail-order houses from the 1920s.

Sights

The **Cape Charles Museum and Welcome Center** (814 Randolph Ave., 757/331-1008, 10 A.M.–2 P.M. Mon.–Fri., 10 A.M.–5 P.M.

Sat., 1–5 P.M. Sun., Apr.–Nov., free) occupies a building that used to be a generator house for Delmarva Power and still has one gigantic generator (which still turns over) embedded in the floor. Old photos, decoys, and boat models trace the history of Cape Charles.

Recreation

Operating out of an old service station next to the

THE CHESAPEAKE BAY BRIDGE-TUNNEL

Stretching across the mouth of the Chesapeake Bay like a gap-toothed smile, this engineering wonder lets thousands of drivers a day save a hundred-mile detour between Hampton Roads and the Eastern Shore. Officially named the Lucius J. Kellam Jr. Bridge-Tunnel, after the Eastern Shore businessman who conceived of it, the longest bridge-tunnel system in the world comprises 17.65 miles of U.S. 13 from Virginia Beach to Cape Charles.

Construction began in 1958 to replace ferry service that had operated since the 1930s. Over the following six years, some 825,000 tons of concrete and 55,000 tons of steel were cast into pilings and sections of roadway on shore, hauled out on barges, and fit together like the world's biggest Lego project. The most impressive feat was the raising of four man-made islands in water averaging 40 feet deep. Each one, large enough to hold Yankee Stadium, serves as one end to two mile-long tunnels sunk beneath the main shipping channels.

Two hundred million dollars later the bridge opened, allowing the first ceremonial vehicle to cross 12 miles of trestled roadway, dip under the bay twice, and pass over two high-clearance bridges near Fisherman Island off Cape Charles. (The idea of one long bridge was scrapped by navy strategists, who said it would be too easy for enemies to destroy and block the navigable lanes with debris during wartime.) In 1965 it was declared one of the Seven Engineering Wonders of the Modern World. In the 1990s, a parallel bridge was constructed to handle future traffic demands. Today, one bridge carries northbound traffic while the other handles southbound traffic.

Total cost: $450 million. In 2006, the bridge-tunnel was destroyed – fictionally – in the movie *Mission: Impossible 3*.

Sea Gull Island, the southernmost of the man-made islands, is home to a simple, inexpensive restaurant (serving all meals), gift shop, and 625-foot fishing pier (757/331-2960) with bait and tackle for sale and rent. Fish-cleaning stations and a certified scale are available and no fishing license is needed. It's a great way to go deep-sea fishing without a boat.

Even though you might not believe that all this thundering traffic is conducive to wildlife viewing, the artificial islands are among the best places in Virginia to watch migratory seabirds in the winter. Scooters, ruddy turnstones, scaup, eiders, and other duck species, including buffleheads, gadwalls, and common goldeneyes, all make appearances in the winter, especially after a hard freeze. Be advised, though, that increased bridge security measures begun in 2005 mean you'll have to arrange for the bird-watching session well ahead of time by submitting $50 and a permit (www.cbbt.com/birding.html). The fee goes to cover the police escort required to accompany your group of no more than 15 people while you're on the island. Another, easier option is to head to the wildlife viewing area north of the Bridge-Tunnel toll plaza on Virginia's Eastern Shore.

The bridge-tunnel, by the way, is a private enterprise, as permitted by Virginia law. A hefty $12 toll is charged each way, with a $17 round-trip option within 24 hours. Contact the bridge authority (757/331-2960, www.cbbt.com) for more information.

Sunset Beach Resort, **SouthEast Expeditions** (32218 Lankford Hwy., 757/331-2680, www .southeastexpeditions.net) runs kayak trips as well as sunset excursions and clamming junkets. Two-hour tours start at $45 per person, half-day tours are $85 per person, and full-day trips are $125 and include lunch. It also rents kayaks by the hour or day and was the first place in the state to offer instruction in the hair-raising sport of kiteboarding (www.gogetlit.com). Imagine strapping your feet onto a floating surfboard and grabbing the reins of an inflatable kite that's big enough to yank you dozens of feet into the air (not to mention pull you along at a swift clip in between jumps), and you have the general idea.

Events

In May, July, and September, Cape Charles holds an **Applaud the Sun Harbor Party** the first Saturday evening of each month June–September to celebrate its location on the largest harbor between Norfolk and Maryland.

Accommodations and Food

The **Sea Gate Bed & Breakfast** (9 Tazewell Ave., 757/331-2206, www.bbhost.com/Seagate, $120–130) is in a lovingly restored 1912 house with four guest rooms. A curving porch wraps around the entire front of the building, which was once split into a duplex. The Peach and Rose Rooms share a balcony with wicker chairs. Corinthian columns flank the foyer of the **Cape Charles House** (645 Tazewell Ave., 757/331-4920, www.capecharleshouse.com), set in a 1912 Colonial Revival frame house with high ceilings and maple plank floors. Five rooms range in price $120–200.

The **Sunset Beach Resort** (32246 Lankford Hwy., 757/331-4786 or 800/899-4786, www.sunsetbeachresortva.com) has 73 rooms ($160–180) and an outdoor pool along with a beachfront café by a small stretch of private beach. In winter, the resort also opens 52 RV campsites for $40 per night. It's located a few miles north of the Bridge-Tunnel entrance on U.S. 13. Approximately 1.5 miles west of U.S. 13 on Route 680, you'll find the **Cherrystone Family Camping & RV Resort**

(757/331-3063, www.cherrystoneva.com), with three pools, a beach, sports courts, and a playground spread over more than 300 acres. They rent sea kayaks, pedalboats, and bikes and have more than 300 campsites for $37–63, plus cabins for $390–975 a night in high season. Sites with a water view cost $5 extra.

There aren't many service stations where you can get a hand-pulled pork barbecue plate and a glass of merlot, but Cape Charles has one. Head back out to U.S. 13 and a little more than four miles south, where (**Sting-Ray's** (26507 Lankford Hwy., 757/331-2505, from 6 A.M. daily) is a local gathering place serving gourmet seafood platters in the back of a big red Exxon station. It may not look like much, but wait until you try the soft-shells and crab imperial, maybe accompanied by a bottle from one of the best wine selections on the Eastern Shore. It also serves inexpensive sandwiches, breakfasts, and the usual ribs and chili ($5–27).

Information

For details on anything else about the town, contact the **Northhampton County Chamber of Commerce** (757/678-0010, www.ccnc chamber.com).

EASTVILLE

In 1766, 10 years before the signing of the Declaration of Independence, the county court of this tiny village—then called Peachburg—declared the Stamp Act of Parliament unconstitutional. By the early 19th century, it boasted 217 inhabitants who, in the words of one visitor, were "not to be surpassed for their morality and hospitality to strangers."

The **Old Courthouse** on Courthouse Square guards the oldest continuous court records in America, which have escaped fire, rot, and rats since they were begun in 1632. The building dates to the turn of the 20th century. Next door, the **Clerk's Office** has a small museum inside, with items including leg irons and a device for measuring slaves' heights. Barred windows mark the **Debtors' Prison**, on Courthouse Road (U.S. 13 Business), built around 1814, with an old whipping post

OFFSHORE EDEN

The Nature Conservancy oversees the outermost fringe of Virginia's Eastern Shore, the largest stretch of unspoiled coastal wilderness in the country. With 38,000 acres spread over 14 barrier islands, the Virginia Coast Reserve has been designated one of the 10 Last Great Places in America by its custodians and an International Biosphere Reserve by the United Nations.

Beaches, lagoons, pine forests, marshes, and scrub woodlands shelter as many as 80,000 pairs of nesting birds at a time, including every species found along Virginia's coast. Visiting is limited to day use, but the boating, bird-watching, and picnicking are unsurpassed. Getting there is the only catch; it requires a boat or canoe. Parramore, Shipshoal, and Revel Islands are closed to the public, and much of Cedar Island remains in private hands.

Check with **The Nature Conservancy** (757/442-3049) for regulations and information. Captain Rick Kellam's **Broadwater Bay Ecotours** (757/442-4363, www.broadwaterbayecotour.com) can be customized to focus on history, nature, or sightseeing. Kellam is a former waterman and marine law enforcement officer (five generations of Kellams lived on Hog Island before the hurricane of 1933 persuaded them to pack up), and he worked for The Nature Conservancy before starting his own tour business – his tours are excellent (half-day $90 pp, full-day $180 pp, half-price for kids under 12).

by the Sea" in an Indian tongue. Wachapreague (WAH-cha-preeg) is a good base for charter fishing or exploring the islands and marshes of the Eastern Shore's Atlantic edge.

Three brothers named Powell established a wharf and shipping firm here in 1872. Weekly freight and passenger steamers left for points north around the turn of the 20th century, when wealthy visiting sportsmen enjoyed a dance hall, pool room, movie houses, and an elegant hotel (which burned in 1978).

Recreation

Ask at the Wachapreague Marina (757/787-4110) or **Captain Zed's Tackle Shop & Marina** (757/789-3222) about fishing charters starting at $500 for flounder and $1,100 for marlin. Four-person 16-foot skiffs are available for rent for $125 per day.

Accommodations and Food

On the waterfront, the **Wachapreague Motel** (1 Main St., 757/787-2105, www.wachapreague.com) has 21 newly renovated rooms, efficiencies, and two-bedroom apartments starting at $90 in season ($65 off-season), as well as a large, refurbished rental house that sleeps 11 ($380). It also books trips with several local charter boats. Across the street is the **Island House Restaurant** (757/787-4242, www.islandhouseentertainment.com, lunch and dinner daily, weekends only in winter), overlooking the marsh across the street and enclosing the self-declared finest raw bar on the Eastern Shore. Platters are $10–19, including great crab cakes and Black Angus steaks.

Events and Information

The **Wachapreague Volunteer Fireman's Carnival** (757/787-2105) comes to town mid-June to mid-July. Several fishing tournaments swing through town as well during the summer; call the Wachapreague Motel for more information.

in front that may make you grateful for the comparatively civilized techniques of modern collection agencies. Ask in the modern Northampton Administration Building (757/678-0440) for keys to these three buildings during business hours.

WACHAPREAGUE

Two hundred folks live in the Flounder Capital of the World, whose name means "Little City

ONANCOCK

One of the Eastern Shore's prettiest towns sits on Onancock Creek near one of the two deepwater harbors on the peninsula. Chock full of 19th-century houses with gingerbread trim and wraparound porches, Onancock (o-NAN-cock) has enough cultural offerings and quiet allure to justify a stay of a weekend or more.

The name, meaning "foggy place" in an Indian language, comes from a native tribe whose King Ekeeks introduced Englishman John Pory to oysters and "batata" (potatoes) in 1621. (After burning his mouth on a steaming tuber, Pory groaned, "I would not give a farthing for a truckload.") the settlement, founded in 1680 as Port Scarburgh, weathered frequent raids by British privateers during the Revolutionary War. Growth arrived with steamships plying the Chesapeake Bay, leaving Onancock one of the largest communities on the Eastern Shore.

For more information, visit the websites www.onancock.com and www.onancock.org.

Sights

On Market Street (Rte. 179) before the center of town stands **Kerr Place** (757/787-8012, www.kerrplace.org, 11 A.M.–4 P.M. Tues.–Sat. Mar.–Dec., $5 pp), one of the Eastern Shore's finest antique manor homes. Built in 1799 by a Scottish merchant, the elegant Federal mansion once presided over an estate of 1,500 acres. It's been restored by the Eastern Shore of Virginia Historical Society, which has set up offices, a museum, and a museum store inside. Intricate woodwork and plaster carvings decorate the walls and ceiling around period artwork and furniture. Notice the false window in the brick facade, included for symmetry.

Shopping

The **Willie Crockett Gallery** (39 Market St., 757/787-2288, www.williecrockett.com) offers nautical-themed works by the Tangier-born artist. Look to **gardenART** (44 King St., 757/787-8818) for plants, flowers, and whimsical garden decor. The funky shop has a friendly Portuguese water dog on hand as a greeter and is situated in a former power plant.

Off U.S. 13 south of Onancock, **Turner Sculpture** (757/787-2818, www

.turnersculpture.com, 9 A.M.–5 P.M. daily) is the largest personal foundry and gallery in the country. Renowned sculptors William and David Turner count the National Audubon Society, the American Museum of Natural History, and the White House among dozens of public commissions for their realistic wildlife bronzes. Here in the gallery, more than 300 different animals are frozen in vivid poses that work especially well for the aquatic creatures—otters, dolphins, humpback whales, and the like. Prices range from $50 for palm-size works into the thousands for larger pieces.

Accommodations and Food

The **Colonial Manor Inn** (84 Market St., 757/787-3521, www.colonialmanorinn.com, $100–140) got its start as a boardinghouse in the 1930s, making it the oldest continually operating inn on the Eastern Shore. Full use of two acres of grounds and full breakfasts served at the huge dining table are included in the price.

Charlotte Heath and Gary Cochran purchased the building that began as the White Hotel in 1907, and turned it into the charming **Charlotte Hotel & Restaurant** (7 North St., 757/787-7400, www.thecharlottehotel.com). Gary made all the beds by hand, and Charlotte's artwork hangs in the dining room. They offer eight guest rooms ($115–160), a dining room (breakfast and dinner Wed.–Sun.), and a full-service bar. All the food is made in-house, with a seasonally changing "creative American" menu of entrées ranging $15–35 for dinner.

Originally built around 1880 as a private residence, the **Inn & Garden Café** (145 Market St., 757/787-8850, www.theinnandgardencafe.com) was entirely renovated in 2004. Four guest suites are $96–130 in season, and the 50-seat fine-dining restaurant (dinner Tues.–Wed. and Fri.–Sat., brunch Sun., $20–32, weekday specials for less) has seating inside or in an enclosed outdoor gazebo overlooking the gardens. Seafood entrées with a Southern flair run $20–28.

Bizotto's Gallery-Caffe (41 Market St., 757/787-3103, lunch Mon.–Sat., dinner daily, closed Sun. off-season) is a gallery for hand-tooled leather handbags and briefcases made by the owner as well as a popular restaurant that's packed at lunchtime. Dishes like veal picatta and filet mignon start at $7 for lunch and $18 for dinner. Another good dining choice is **Mallard's on the Wharf** (2 Market St., 757/787-8558, lunch and dinner daily). It's inside the venerable Hopkins Bros. Store, which began in 1842 as a feed and farm store and the village post office, making it one of the oldest general stores on the East Coast. Soups, salads, and sandwiches are $7–11, and entrées like broiled rockfish are $15–28. It's part of chef Johnny Mo's local restaurant portfolio, which also includes Mallard's Sidewalk Café in Accomac.

ONANCOCK TO CHINCOTEAGUE
Accomac
A wealth of Colonial architecture fills the tree-shaded streets in this historic burg, founded as Drummondtown in the 18th century. On Courthouse Green stands the early-1900s **Courthouse** next to the Victorian brick **Clerk's Office,** where the Accomac County Orders of 1714–1717 bear the vitriolic inscription "God Damn the King" instead of the more traditional "God Save the King."

Elaborate paintings inside the Greek Revival **St. James Episcopal Church** (built in 1838) simulate columns, doors, and arches. Call 757/789-3247 to arrange a visit to the 1782 **Debtors' Prison,** which housed the financially irresponsible and unlucky until it was rendered obsolete in 1849 by a state law that abolished imprisonment for debt. It's run by the Association for the Preservation of Virginia Antiquities.

Parksley
The **Eastern Shore Railway Museum** (18468 Dunne Ave., 757/665-7245, 10 A.M.–4 P.M. Mon.–Sat., 1–4 P.M. Sun., $2 adults, free children under 12) starts with a gift shop and

collection of antique cars in the 1906 New York, Philadelphia, and Norfolk Railroad passenger station. An original freight station across the yard holds uniforms, maps, and lanterns from back when railroads were the lifeline of the Eastern Shore, while the yard is full of dining cars and cabooses from the Richmond, Fredericksburg & Potomac, Norfolk & Western, and Wabash lines. The museum is two miles west of U.S. 13 on VA 176 (Parksley Rd.).

CHINCOTEAGUE
From killdeer nesting in parking lots to gales that redefine the sandy shoreline, life on Chincoteague Island is shaped by the natural world. Known for its annual pony swim and auction, the largest community on the Eastern Shore combines a seasonal beach resort with a timeless offshore sanctuary, home to plenty of coastal life besides the famous fillies.

History
The story goes that on October 25, 1662, this island, sandwiched between the mainland and Assateague, was granted to Capt. William Whitington by Wachawampe, emperor of the Gingo Teagues. Over time the tribe's name would evolve into Chincoteague (SHINK-a-teeg), meaning "Beautiful Land Across the Water." A tiny settlement was destroyed by a tidal wave that swept over both islands in 1821, but the area gradually resettled over the next decades.

In 1861, a 132–2 vote to remain part of the Union set Chincoteague against the rest of its parent state. Several attempts by mainlanders to storm the island were repelled. The railroad arrived in 1876, ending an era of lawlessness, illiteracy, and bare feet with the introduction of schools, churches, a newspaper, and new homes.

Incorporated as a town in 1908, Chincoteague was connected to the mainland by an automobile causeway in 1922. Marguerite Henry's 1947 book, *Misty of Chincoteague,* propelled the town into the collective imagination of children worldwide as only a book about horses can. Many local residents appeared in the movie made from the children's story in the 1960s, and the town's name has been synonymous with ponies on the beach ever since.

Orientation

The town of Chincoteague occupies most of the island of the same name, connected to the mainland and U.S. 13 by Route 175. A long, straight causeway crosses marshland and a drawbridge to Main Street, running the length of the island's western shore. Head north (left) on Main Street for a few blocks and turn east (right) onto Maddox Boulevard, where signs lead to the visitors center and the Chincoteague National Wildlife Refuge.

Sights

The world's only oyster museum is right here in Chincoteague. The **Oyster and Maritime Museum** (7125 Maddox Blvd., 757/336-6117, 10 a.m.–5 p.m. daily in season, $4 adults, $2 children) holds the huge lens from the Assateague Island Lighthouse and exhibits on the history of the local oyster industry.

Fishing

Dozens of places in Chincoteague rent boats and fishing tackle for visitors interested in exploring the fringes of Chincoteague Bay. Expect to pay $50–75 per day for a midsized fishing boat for 3–4 people and upwards of $100 for a 12-person pontoon boat for four hours. Rods and reels, crab pots, and clam rakes are $5–10 per day. Try **Barnacle Bill's Bait & Tackle** (3691 Main St., 757/336-5920, www.chincoteague.com/barnaclebills), which runs scenic tours starting at $15 per person, or **Capt. Bob's Marina** (2477 Main St., 757/336-6654, www.captbobs-marina.com). **Snug Harbor Resort** (7536 East Side Rd., 757/336-6176) rents boats, canoes, kayaks, and personal watercraft starting at $29 per boat for a half day, $39 per boat for a full day.

Charters let you venture offshore for the big ones: tuna, marlin, swordfish, and shark. Two- to four-hour bay fishing trips run about $50 including all bait and tackle, with offshore trips varying in price depending on the size of the party and what you're after. Captain Fred Gilman of **Reel Time Charters** (757/336-2236, www.chincoteague.com/reeltime) offers offshore, big game, and wreck fishing from a 33-foot sportfishing boat. The *Chincoteague View* (757/336-6861, www.chincoteague.com/cview) is a pontoon boat out of Curtis Merrit Harbor that's available for morning or afternoon fishing charters after flounder, bluefish, sea bass, and other species.

Tours and Excursions

Captain Barry's Back Bay Cruises (6262 Marlin St., 757/336-6508, www.captainbarry.net) leave from the dock at the Chincoteague Inn Restaurant for early-morning bird-watching ($25 pp) and half-day Coastal Encounters for $45 per person, with historical tidbits and natural-history stops galore. Reservations are required. The *Linda J* (757/336-6214, http://mysite.verizon.net/lindajcharters) is a 24-foot pontoon boat that can be booked for sightseeing and nature trips for $30 per person.

No less than six tours a day are on the roster for the *Assateague Explorer* (757/336-5956 or 866/766-9794, www.assateagueisland.com/explorer.htm), including pony-spotting, bird-watching, fishing, and sunset cruises ($40 adults, $30 children under 12), leaving from Curtis Merritt Harbor.

Other Recreation

If you can't visit during the Pony Roundup, you can still get a close-up view at the **Chincoteague Pony Centre** (6417 Carriage Dr., 757/336-2776, www.chincoteague.com/ponycentre), offering afternoon pony rides daily. Despite the name, **Jus' Bikes** (6527 Maddox Blvd., 757/336-6700) rents bikes (single and tandem) but also scooters, mopeds, kiddie carts, and helmets.

Shopping

Another unmistakable sign of beach resorts is dozens of stores selling everything from crafts, dolls, and candles to framed seascapes and Christmas goodies in July, and Chincoteague is no exception. Ronald Justis's **Decoys Decoys Decoys** (4039 Main St., 757/336-1402) offers one of the largest selections on the East Coast. The **Main Street Shop Coffeehouse** (4288 Main St., 757/336-6782) has an eclectic selection of artwork and great coffee. Local artist Nancy West has oil paintings, woven clothing, and unique jewelry at **Island Arts** (6196 Maddox Blvd., 757/336-3113), while Welsh native Hal Lott sells silk-screens through **Lott's Arts & Things** (4281 Main St., 757/336-5773).

Events

Many of Chincoteague's annual events require advance tickets; call the Chincoteague Chamber of Commerce for information.

Bring a bib to the **Seafood Festival** at Tom's Cove Campground the first Wednesday in May. All you can eat of bushels of raw oysters, shoals of fish, and tens of thousands of clams are yours for the price of a ticket, but the event is popular, so you have to buy that ticket in advance from the Eastern Shore Chamber of Commerce (757/787-2460). If you can, return for the **Blessing of the Fleet** at the end of the month, where local ministers ask for local watermen to come home safe with plenty of fish.

The **Pony Roundup and Swim** is Chincoteague's biggest happening and one of the largest on the Virginia coast. Held since 1925, this event is preceded by the Fireman's Carnival on multiple weekends (Friday and Saturday evenings) throughout July. At the end of the month, members of the Chincoteague Volunteer Fire Company dress up as cowboys and round up the herd of wild ponies that lives in the Chincoteague National Wildlife Refuge. After swimming across the channel, the horses step ashore at Memorial Park at the southern end of the island. Here they're penned until the famous auction, attended by 50,000 or more people. The pony auction began in 1925 as a fundraiser for the Chincoteague Volunteer Fire Department, and continues in this capacity today. It also helps control the size of the herd. Each pony has already been cleared for

travel by veterinarians, so if you succumb and buy one, you can take it right home. This event fills the town to capacity, so book accommodations well in advance. The **Chincoteague Blueberry Festival** happens at the beginning of Pony Penning Week.

October brings more food festivals. First the **Chincoteague Island Oyster Festival** rolls into town. It's been held since 1972 and brings all the oysters you can eat ($35 pp), in every variety imaginable, to the Maddox Family Campground, along with tons of other food and musical entertainment (buy tickets early; 757/336-6161). Then the **Chili & Chowder Cookoff** arrives midmonth to the town's waterfront park.

Accommodations

As befits a seasonal resort town, many hotels in Chincoteague close or drop their prices by as much as half in the off-season.

The T-shaped **1848 Island Manor House** (4160 Main St., 757/336-5436 or 800/852-1505, www.islandmanor.com, $125–215) was built by a local Union surgeon and a postmaster who married a pair of sisters. Apparently the wives didn't get along under the same roof, prompting their husbands to split the house in two. It's since been rejoined and decorated in Federal style. All lodgings come with a full Southern-style breakfast and trail mix, and special romantic getaway packages are offered.

◖ **Miss Molly's Inn** (4141 Main St., 757/336-6686 or 800/221-5620, www.missmollys-inn.com, $110–180) occupies a Victorian home built in 1886 by J. T. Rowley for his daughter Molly, who lived there until age 84. Marguerite Henry stayed here while writing *Misty of Chincoteague,* and the room has since been named after her. Prices include full breakfasts in the gazebo and scones at teatime. The same owners also operate the **Channel Bass Inn** (6228 Church St., 757/336-6148 or 800/249-0818, www.channelbass-inn.com, $125–225), dating to 1892. Some of the five rooms and one suite have a view of the Chesapeake Bay, and the public is welcome to stop by for Barbara's famous scones at afternoon tea in the Tea Room—just call ahead for reservations.

A wraparound veranda and scallop shingles adorn **The Watson House** (4240 Main St., 757/336-1564 or 800/336-6787, www.watson house.com, $130–175), built in 1898 by David Robert Watson. Guests have access to complimentary bicycles and beach chairs.

A hot tub, crabbing dock, and solarium are only some of the amenities at the **Waterside Inn** (3761 S. Main St., 877/870-3434, www .watersidemotorinn.com, $135–160). The **Refuge Inn** (7058 Maddox Blvd., 757/336-5511 or 888/257-0038, www.refugeinn.com) has rooms for $90–190 and suites for $180–320, depending on the season, as well as a three-bedroom Cape Cod–style cottage on the north end of the island, where ponies sometimes graze just beyond the fence ($585 for three nights or $1,400 per week).

Camping
The **Maddox Family Campground** (6742 Maddox Blvd., 757/336-3111, www.chinco teague.com/maddox) has 550 sites open March–November for $37–42, depending on whether you want hookups. It also offers a pool, showers, and crabbing equipment and takes reservations. **Tom's Cove Campground** (8128 Beebe Rd., 757/336-6498, www.tomscovepark.com) has waterfront sites within sight of the pony swim for $31–50, open March–November, along with three fishing piers and an Olympic-sized pool. A site at the **Pine Grove Campground** (5283 Deep Hole Rd., 757/336-5200, www .pinegrovecampground.com) is $30–40 during the April–November camping season. It has all the amenities, as well as a small motel (open May–Oct., $50–85), two waterfront cottages nearby ($1,600–1,800/week), and six ponds that are popular with birds.

Food
Dining in Chincoteague is a lesson in convergent evolution: Most of the 23 restaurants are named after someone and offer family-style food, usually seafood, for all meals daily. Many are only open Memorial Day to Labor Day, and most of the rest limit their hours in the off-season. Steak, seafood, and chicken entrées tend to run $12–17.

Popular spots include **Etta's Channel Side Restaurant** (7452 East Side Dr., 757/336-5644, dinner daily, from noon Sun.) and **Mr. Baldy's Family Restaurant** (3441 Ridge Rd., 757/336-1198). **AJ's on the Creek** (6585 Maddox Blvd., 757/336-5888, lunch and dinner Mon.–Sat.) is an intimate, romantic place with some of the better seafood in town. It also serves steaks and pasta and has a screened-in porch.

Don's Seafood Restaurant (4113 Main St., 757/336-5715, lunch and dinner daily) also has a lounge with a raw bar and dancing past midnight. Not to be outdone, **Bill's Seafood Restaurant** (4040 Main St., 757/336-5831, all meals daily) has all the surf and turf you could hope to eat, and gets the locals' vote (dinner entrées $13–30).

Steamers (6251 Maddox Blvd., 757/336-5300, dinner daily) is an informal seafood joint popular with tourists and locals and is almost always packed in season. All-you-can-eat feasts start in the low $20s and include soup, salads, biscuits, hush puppies, corn on the cob, sweet potatoes, and the seafood of your choice. Butcher paper and a garbage can for every table keeps the mess to a minimum.

Information
The Chincoteague Chamber of Commerce operates a **visitors center** (6733 Maddox Blvd., 757/336-6161, www.chincoteaguechamber .com, 8:30 A.M.–4:30 P.M. Mon.–Sat.) in a traffic circle about one mile west of the bridge to Assateague Island. For more information, visit the website www.chincoteague.com.

Near Chincoteague
The National Advisory Committee on Aeronautics (NACA) opened an aeronautical research center at Wallops Island in 1945. NACA became a full federal agency, the National Aeronautics and Space Administration (NASA), in 1958, and over the years, the **Wallops Flight Facility** has tested

and launched thousands of orbital and suborbital rockets and balloons. An agreement also allows launches of commercial satellites. The agency runs a **visitors center** (757/824-2298 or 757/824-1344, 10 A.M.–4 P.M. daily July–Aug., Thurs.–Mon. off-season, free), tracing the history of flight, rockets, and space travel through video displays, photos, and real relics of the space program. Space-suit demonstrations and launchings of model rockets take place during the summer. Call ahead for a launch schedule, although many rockets launched from here aren't all that big or impressive.

◖ CHINCOTEAGUE NATIONAL WILDLIFE REFUGE AND ASSATEAGUE ISLAND

Assateague Island, a thin ribbon of sand 37 miles long, extends from Ocean City, Maryland, to just past Chincoteague Island. In numerous places along the way its solitude is in striking juxtaposition to both resorts. The entire spit has been designated a National Seashore, and Virginia's end of the island was set aside in 1943 as the Chincoteague National Wildlife Refuge to protect dwindling habitat for migrating snow geese.

There's much more to the fishhook tip of sand than the graceful white birds with black wingtips, though. Virginia's portion of the wild pony herd draws plenty of visitors, while enough birds pass through during migrating season to guarantee additions to most birdwatchers' life lists. Even though they're not open to camping on this end of the island, 10 miles of wild oceanside beaches offer wave-soothed solitude for hikers who venture off the more popular beaches.

Habitats

Tidal salt marshes and mudflats line the ragged landward side of the island, facing Chincoteague Island and Chincoteague Bay. Pine and hardwood forests fill the interior, dotted with pools and the large bight of Toms Cove at the southernmost end. The smooth Atlantic edge is almost pure sand, which is slowly being pushed southward by the endless caress of the ocean.

Assateague Island, where the Chincoteague National Wildlife Refuge is located, faces the open Atlantic, with sea breezes and ocean waves.

Species

More than 300 species of **birds** depend on the rich harvest of plants, mollusks, insects, and crustaceans provided by Assateague Island's freshwater impoundments, marshes, mudflats, tidal pools, and maritime forests. Herons, egrets, gulls, terns, and sandpipers arrive in the summer, followed in the fall by migrating shorebirds and peregrine falcons, which are easier to spot on Assateague than almost anywhere else on the East Coast. Migrating waterfowl, including mallards, pintails, black ducks, Canada geese, and greater snow geese, take advantage of the island's mild winter climate during their thousand-mile journeys. Keep an ear out for the distinctive call of the willet, and be aware of area closures (usually most of Toms Cove Hook) to protect the nesting sites of the threatened piping plover.

Most famous of Assateague's 44 mammal species are undoubtedly the **wild ponies,** separated into two herds by a fence at the Maryland state line. The Virginia herd is owned by the Chincoteague Volunteer Fire Company and allowed to graze on federal land by special permit. It's fun to hear the legend that they swam ashore from a shipwrecked Spanish galleon, but it's more probable (and prosaic) that they're the descendants of herds hidden on the island in the 17th century by mainland colonists trying to avoid livestock taxes. This means they're actually stunted horses, not true ponies.

With their shaggy manes and stubby legs, they look cute enough to pet, which many people do—bad idea. These are not tame horses, and visitors get bitten and kicked every year and promptly blame the refuge staff for their own foolishness. The horses' short stature and their bloated bellies, which can't handle human handouts, are most likely the result of generations of salty marsh grass and brackish water.

Your best chance of spotting them is from the Woodland Trail in Black Duck Marsh, but you might bump into a few just about anywhere. While the Maryland herd grazes at large, the Virginia herd grazes in two fenced compartments, to keep them out of sensitive habitats and away from people.

© KATIE GITHENS

With stubby legs and shaggy manes, the famous Chincoteague wild ponies are cute – but remember to give them a wide berth.

Great white egrets can be found fishing in the ditches around Assateague Island.

A quarter-mile hike up a sandy rise brings you to the Assateague Island Lighthouse.

A small herd of Asian **sika deer**—actually an elk species—was released by a Boy Scout troop in 1923 at the northern end of the island, and the deer now outnumber the native **white-tailed deer.** If you come across a large, relatively unfazed rodent with a big bushy tail, it's probably an endangered **Delmarva Peninsula fox squirrel.**

Visiting the Refuge

The refuge encompasses the Virginia portion of the **Assateague Island National Seashore** (757/336-6577 or 410/641-1441, www.nps .gov/asis). (To further complicate things, part of the Maryland section of the seashore is also a state park.) The refuge entrance, at the end of Maddox Boulevard, is open 5 A.M.–10 P.M. daily in season for $5 per car. The U.S. Fish and Wildlife Service operates the **Herbert H. Bateman Center** (757/336-6122, http:// chinco.fws.gov, 9 A.M.–5 P.M. daily in summer, until 4 P.M. rest of year), with wildlife information, trail brochures, and schedules of interpretive activities. Be sure to pay homage to the **Assateague Island Lighthouse,** painted in jaunty red and white stripes and standing 142 feet tall. Completed in 1867, the lighthouse is still in use today, warning ships of shoals that once sank President Harrison's yacht. The beams are visible up to 22 nautical miles offshore.

Parts of the beach are open to surfing, fishing, swimming, clamming, and crabbing. Fifteen miles of trails include the 1.6-mile Woodland Trail to an overlook over pony-favored Black Duck Marsh; the 3.2-mile Wildlife Loop, open to vehicles 3 P.M.–dusk; and the Toms Cove Nature Trail, out along the southern tail. Miles of untracked beach stretch north from the National Park Service's **Toms Cove Visitor Center** (757/336-6577, 9 A.M.–5 P.M. daily in summer, until 4 P.M. rest of year), at the entrance to Toms Cove Hook. Inside the visitors center, kids will want to explore the aquarium and touch tank. Back outside, cyclists are welcome on paved trails. Boaters should check ahead of time for permitted landing sites.

Camping isn't allowed in the Virginia end of the refuge, but it is north of the Maryland border. You can pick up backcountry permits ($5) at Toms Cove, but the closest campsite is a 12-mile paddle or hike over sand while carrying drinking water and provisions for the trip. From the Maryland side, the distance is less daunting, only two miles away, and car camping is also available (410/641-3030, www.nps.gov/asis, $16–20). Dog owners take note: Pets are *only* permitted in the Maryland campground in the national wildlife refuge. No dogs are allowed anywhere on the Virginia side—not even inside cars.

Across the state line, **Assateague State Park** (410/641-2120 or 888/432-2267, www.dnr.state.md.us/publiclands/eastern/assateague.html, $4 pp) also has campsites for $30–40 from May to October.

Both the Park Service and the U.S. Fish and Wildlife Service offer naturalist programs in the refuge daily during summer and on spring and fall weekends. Annual events start with the **International Migratory Bird Celebration** in May, with guided walks, speakers, and workshops, and continue through **National Wildlife Refuge Week** in October. **Waterfowl Week,** in late November during the southward migration of Canada and snow geese, is the only time visitors can drive to the northern end of the refuge via the Northern Service Road.

The **Assateague Coastal Trust** (410/629-1538, www.actforbays.org) is a grassroots nonprofit organization dedicated to preserving Assateague Island and its surrounding ecosystem through outreach programs and advocacy efforts. It organizes occasional conferences, lectures, and workshops.

◖ TANGIER ISLAND

Only 10 or so miles of Chesapeake chop from the mainland, Tangier is decades away from even the atavistic air of the Eastern Shore. The insularity of this tight little fishing community is something you don't come across every day. The pace of life is a little different and the accent hard to place, making a visit as much a cultural experience as a sightseeing jaunt. Even

THE TOWN THAT TURNED PAUL NEWMAN DOWN

The Great Movie Controversy of 1998 showed clearly that increasing tourism hasn't changed the stubbornly independent local attitude of Tangier all that much.

Actor Paul Newman had selected Tangier as the perfect place to film *Message in a Bottle*, a movie starring himself and Kevin Costner. Everything looked great until a core of conservative, born-again Christians on the town council forced a last-minute change of plans. Despite a petition bearing 200 names, the possibility of $23,000 worth of repairs to the town dock, and work for hundreds of hard-up island residents, a 6-0 vote said that the PG-13 script, with its profanity, premarital sex, and alcohol, was inconsistent with community values and therefore unwelcome.

Many indignant islanders pointed out that swearing, procreating, and even illicit drinking all occurred on Tangier – and that legions of locals had taken the boat to Salisbury, Maryland, to see the disaster epic *Titanic*. But the arguments fell on deaf ears, and Newman, who had scoped out the island incognito, had to look elsewhere for a film site.

in a state that has as many curious nooks as Virginia does, Tangier stands out.

History

Indians fished and hunted on the island for centuries, but Tangier wasn't "discovered" by Europeans—Captain John Smith, to be precise—and named until 1608. The first settlement came in 1686, after native tribes, according to a (probably bogus) legend, sold the island for two overcoats. Cornishman John Crockett, along with his eight sons and their families, was the first to arrive. By the 19th century, the island was home to 100 residents, half of them Crocketts, who made a living fishing and grazing livestock.

The outside world intruded during the Revolutionary War, when British troops used the island as a base for raiding American ships. During the War of 1812, 12,000 more redcoats stood under the pines in preparation for an attack on Fort McHenry. Local reverend Joshua Thomas harangued the invaders, claiming that the word from above was that they could not take Baltimore. (He was right.) In 1814, Francis Scott Key boarded a British boat on Tangier to negotiate the release of an American prisoner. During his voyage, Key witnessed the American flag "gallantly streaming" through the Battle of Baltimore, inspiring him to write what would become "the Star-Spangled Banner."

A cholera outbreak in 1866 forced an almost total evacuation of the island, and a huge storm in 1933 inundated everything on the low-lying island but the top floors of houses. Three years later, the Army Air Corps had to drop supplies onto the school playground when the "Big Freeze" clogged the entire northern bay with a foot of ice. Electricity arrived in 1946, and satellite dishes have begun sprouting in the last decade or two.

Tangier Today

A little more than five square miles in area, the island consists of three inhabited "ridges," none more than five feet above the Chesapeake waterline, which are split by canals and connected by bridges. Most is marsh and wetlands, hunting grounds for Virginia rails, muskrats, herons, and egrets. About 530 people currently live on Tangier—fewer than half as many as did at the turn of the 20th century—and most are related. One-third are Crocketts, with the names of other settlers including Pruitt, Dise, Parks, and Wheatley covering most of the remainder. Crabbing and clamming sustain the community, which is still considered the "softshell capital of the world." Men leave before dawn to check the farms alongshore where the famous local crabs are raised.

Tangier has always been a tightly knit community. In the early 1900s, a book by resident Thomas Crockett rattled so many local skeletons that his descendants later gathered up and destroyed as many copies as they could find. During a World War I visit, president Woodrow Wilson found Tangier's doors locked when islanders suspected his aides of being a German raiding party off a submarine. When Accomack County officials sent over a metal jail in the 1930s, island residents threw it into the water, saying they had no need for one.

A peculiar accent, the product of generations of isolation, evokes England's West Country, turning "time" into "toime" and "mind" into "moind." Front yards (the highest ground on the island) are often crowded with graves and headstones, some centuries old, and highly religious roots continue to sprout—a 1995 revival left one-third of the population born-again Christians. All children attend one school, rebuilt in the mid-1990s, which consistently has the highest percentage of graduates (sometimes six out of six) going on to college in the state. Health care comes in the form of mainland physicians who come twice a week, and dentists and optometrists visit monthly.

Everyone knows each other, of course, and welcomes visitors with a wave from golf carts, bright cruiser bicycles, and a handful of cars and trucks. Stacked crab pots fill backyards lined with chain-link fences, and motorboats zoom around the wharf area, a maze of pilings, crab shanties, and trays called "peeler boxes" where crabs are held until they shed their shells.

Recreation

The Sunset Inn rents **golf carts** ($25 half-day, $50 overnight), and the Waterfront Restaurant rents **bicycles** ($5 per day), which can be left sitting around anywhere (where's a thief going to go?). Head to the south end of the island for a nice beach.

The Tangier Island Museum has about a dozen **kayaks** available for visitors to borrow for free, as well as maps of five suggested routes to explore the island by sea. For information on **watermen's tours** around the island, contact Denny Crockett (757/891-2331) or James Eskridge (757/891-2900).

Accommodations and Food

Because lodging options are limited, reservations are essential on Tangier. Alcohol is technically forbidden on the island. Shirley and Wallace Pruitt run **Shirley's Bay View Inn** (16408 West Ridge Rd., 757/891-2396, www.tangierisland.net, $125–140). Wallace was born in the 1806 house, which has a wraparound porch and plantings in abundance. Two rooms in the house and nine cottages behind are open year-round, with air-conditioning, cable TV, and breakfast included. Grace and Jim Brown's **Sunset Inn** (757/891-2535), also on Ridge Road at the south end near the beach, has cottages for $115–130 including breakfast. They also rent golf carts for getting around the island.

Hilda Crockett's Chesapeake House (757/891-2331, www.chesapeakehouse tangier.com) is in town a few blocks south of the church. This local legend, open since 1939, offers rooms in season for $135–145 including breakfast. The restaurant is also open to the public, serving all-you-can-eat meals for $9 (breakfast) and $22 (lunch and dinner) daily. (Children eat for $5–10.)

Lorraine's Seafood & Sandwich Shop (4417 Chambers Ln., 757/891-2225, all meals Mon.–Sat., lunch Sun.) is one of the few restaurants on the island open year-round, serving subs, pizza, and seafood ($5–11). Near the docks are the **Fisherman's Corner Restaurant** (757/891-2900, lunch daily, dinner Mon.–Sat., May–Sept.) and the **Waterfront Restaurant** (lunch daily May–Oct., 757/891-2248), both serving fresh seafood in season. Sandwiches are $6–12, and seafood plates are $10–26—nothing fancy, but as fresh as it comes. The Waterfront also rents bikes for $5 per day.

Information

Tangier doesn't have a centralized tourism body, but the **Tangier Island History Museum and Interpretative Cultural Center** (16215 Main Rd., 302/234-1660, www.tangier historymuseum.org, 11 A.M.–4 P.M. daily) comes close. Swing by the museum for a quick orientation when you arrive.

Getting There

Several tourist ferries run May through October. **Tangier & Rappahannock Cruises** (804/453-2628, www.tangiercruise.com) sends the *Chesapeake Breeze* from the Buzzard's Point Marina near Reedville, Virginia, at 10 A.M. daily May–October, returning at 4 P.M. ($25 adults, $13 children for day trips, $30 adults, $15 children for overnight stays). Phone reservations are a must in the summer.

The modern 300-passenger **Stephen Thomas** (410/968-2338) departs Crisfield, Maryland, at 12:30 P.M. daily May–October, returning at 4 P.M. Tickets are $25 per person for same-day round-trip, $35 per person for overnight.

The 36-foot **Joyce Marie II** (757/891-2505) leaves from Onancock at 10 A.M. Tuesday–Sunday May–October, returning at 4:30 P.M. ($25 pp round-trip). The **Courtney Thomas,** aka "the mail boat," runs year-round ferry service in addition to being Tangier Island's postal service. It leaves Crisfield, Maryland, at 12:30 P.M. Monday–Saturday, and departs Tangier Island at 8 A.M. (no Sunday travel). Call for rates (757/891-2240).

CRAB LINGO

Backfin: large fin containing choice meat
Buster: crab within hours of shedding
Doubler: male and female crab caught in mating embrace
Jimmy: legal-size male
Peeler: crab ready to molt
Pot: crab trap
Sook: mature female

www.moon.com

DESTINATIONS | ACTIVITIES | BLOGS | MAPS | BOOKS

MOON.COM is ready to help plan your next trip! Filled with fresh trip ideas and strategies, author interviews, informative travel blogs, a detailed map library, and descriptions of all the Moon guidebooks, Moon.com is all you need to get out and explore the world—or even places in your own backyard. While at Moon.com, sign up for our monthly e-newsletter for updates on new releases, travel tips, and expert advice from our on-the-go Moon authors. As always, when you travel with Moon, expect an experience that is uncommon and truly unique.

MOON IS ON FACEBOOK—BECOME A FAN!
JOIN THE MOON PHOTO GROUP ON FLICKR

MAP SYMBOLS

▦ Expressway	**C**	Highlight	✈	Airport	**M**	Metro
Primary Road	○	City/Town	✕	Airfield	**P**	Parking Area
Secondary Road	◉	State Capital	▲	Mountain	⚲	Golf Course
Unpaved Road	⊛	National Capital	✦	Unique Natural Feature	⛪	Church
Trail	★	Point of Interest	⤜	Waterfall	⛽	Gas Station
Ferry	•	Accommodation	⚑	Park		Glacier
Railroad	▼	Restaurant/Bar	⬛	Trailhead		Mangrove
Pedestrian Walkway	■	Other Location	⛷	Skiing Area		Reef
Stairs	⋀	Campground	⚔	Battlefield		Swamp

CONVERSION TABLES

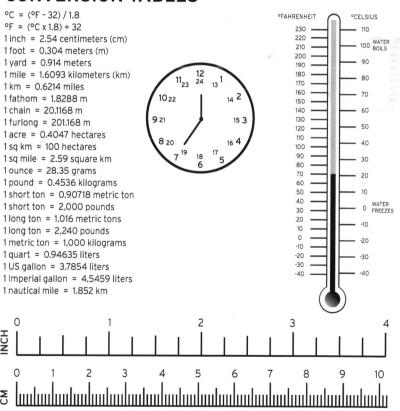

°C = (°F – 32) / 1.8
°F = (°C x 1.8) + 32
1 inch = 2.54 centimeters (cm)
1 foot = 0.304 meters (m)
1 yard = 0.914 meters
1 mile = 1.6093 kilometers (km)
1 km = 0.6214 miles
1 fathom = 1.8288 m
1 chain = 20.1168 m
1 furlong = 201.168 m
1 acre = 0.4047 hectares
1 sq km = 100 hectares
1 sq mile = 2.59 square km
1 ounce = 28.35 grams
1 pound = 0.4536 kilograms
1 short ton = 0.90718 metric ton
1 short ton = 2,000 pounds
1 long ton = 1.016 metric tons
1 long ton = 2,240 pounds
1 metric ton = 1,000 kilograms
1 quart = 0.94635 liters
1 US gallon = 3.7854 liters
1 Imperial gallon = 4.5459 liters
1 nautical mile = 1.852 km

MOON SPOTLIGHT VIRGINIA COAST
Avalon Travel
a member of the Perseus Books Group
1700 Fourth Street
Berkeley, CA 94710, USA
www.moon.com

Editor and Series Manager: Kathryn Ettinger
Copy Editor: Amy Scott
Graphics Coordinator: Elizabeth Jang
Production Coordinator: Elizabeth Jang
Cover Designer: Kathryn Osgood
Map Editor: Albert Angulo
Cartographers: Kat Bennett, Allison Rawley

ISBN: 978-1-59880-682-3

Front cover photo: horse at Assateague Island National
Seashore © Mastudio / Dreamstime.com
Title page photo: wagon ride in Colonial Williamsburg
© Katie Githens

Printed in the United States

ABOUT THE AUTHOR

Katie Githens

Travel writer Katie Githens already had her nose to the ground, so to speak, exploring the best of Virginia when she started her research for *Moon Spotlight Virginia Coast*. Her first book, *The Dog Lover's Companion to Washington DC* (which includes northern Virginia in its coverage), was still hot off the presses when she set off to explore the Virginia Coast.

Katie learned a few things during her travels: namely, that bluegrass is soul music; that she would have aced American history if she grew up here; and that knowing how to drive on winding country roads in winter is a very, very useful skill to have.

While doing the footwork for *Moon Spotlight Virginia Coast*, Katie kept one eye peeled for outdoor adventure. She loves nothing more than a good, long trail run, except maybe a farmers market to stop at for breakfast when she's done.

Before moving to Arlington County in 2005, Katie wrapped up a journalism degree from beachfront Pepperdine University and honed her writing skills at *The Aspen Times* and *Los Angeles Sports & Fitness* magazine. When she's not researching a project that puts her behind the wheel or holding a leash, Katie is behind a desk as a writer and editor in support of the U.S. Environmental Protection Agency. She lives in Arlington with her husband, Mike Githens, and her dog and frequent travel companion, Denali.